ΟΤ A BED FOR ΙGHT

THE STORY OF TRUST

ΟΤ A BED FOR ΙGHT

)ublin
aile Átha (

ALICE LEAHY AND ANNE DEMPSEY

WE ACKNOWLEDGE WITH THANKS THE FINANCIAL
CONTRIBUTION OF THE BRYAN GUINNESS CHARITABLE
TRUST AND THE ENCOURAGEMENT OF FAMILY AND FRIENDS

First published in 1995 by
Marino Books
An imprint of Mercier Press
16 Hume Street Dublin 2

Trade enquiries to Mercier Press
PO Box 5, 5 French Church Street, Cork

A Marino Original

© Alice Leahy and Anne Dempsey 1995

ISBN 1 86023 024 5
10 9 8 7 6 5 4 3 2 1

A CIP record for this title is available
from the British Library

Cover photo by Derek Speirs/ Report
of Alice with Marese, one of the
women with whom she works
Cover design by Bluett
Set by Richard Parfrey
Printed in Ireland by ColourBooks,
Baldoyle Industrial Estate, Dublin 13

The Publishers acknowledge with
gratitude the financial assistance of
the Bryan Guinness Charitable Trust.

TO PAULINE, MARTIN, JOHN . . . AND ALL THE OTHER
HOMELESS PEOPLE WHOSE LIVES AND DEATHS ARE A
CONSTANT CHALLENGE

The names of some of the private individuals who play a part in this story have been changed.

CONTENTS

Foreword by Maeve Binchy   7
Introduction by Alice Leahy   11

 1 A Day in the Life of Trust   17
 2 Early Days – Alice   25
 3 Early Days – Paul   32
 4 Moving to Dublin – Alice   36
 5 Tragedy – Paul   45
 6 Disenchantment –
    Edging into Social Work – Alice   53
 7 A Stint with Simon – Alice   62
 8 Establishing Trust – Alice   70
 9 A Pattern of Behaviour – Paul   84
10 The 1980s – Alice   90
11 The Psychiatric Merry-Go-Round – Paul   105
12 A Journey in Trust (1)   114
13 A Journey in Trust (2)   126
14 A Spiritual Experience – Paul   135
15 Women and Homelessness   145
16 Health and Homelessness – an Overview   156
17 An End to Running – Paul   169
18 The 1990s   178
    Conclusion   192

FOREWORD

MAEVE BINCHY

There are dozens of Dublins and we all think we know our own. But sometimes we can be jolted into a realisation that we don't know our city at all. All around us there can move backwards and forwards people whose lives have a different heartbeat, whose hopes and dreams and expectations are wildly far from our own.

Alice Leahy and Anne Dempsey, in their picture of the shifting, changing, homeless population of the city, may manage to open the eyes of their fellow Dubliners and make us look with more generous and thoughtful eyes on those who share our streets and parks and the banks beside our river and our canals. The stories that unfold are not meant to make us guilty about those who do have a peaceful place to rest at night; it's more a matter of killing the stereotype of the homeless. They are not all old, withdrawn, eccentric and reclusive. They come from everywhere, those who need a bed for the night. But mainly their needs are much more complex.

The story is written with such a mixture of compassion and sheer matter of factness that you really begin to share the lives of those whom fate has sent in so many directions. It is clear that homelessness can have its own rhythm and purpose. Days do not drift by. There is a reason and a schedule in lives that are lived at a different pace. There are lists of stopping places, the hostels, the centres, the hospitals, the meeting places, the drinking places. There are pen pictures which would cheer you for ever because of the huge survival and imagination of the spirit, and others that would make you despair of the cruelty that humans can inflict on other humans by such neglect and slights.

There are days spent in court where the law struggles to be fair but seems to have a terrible inevitability about it, as if it were all a ritual dance, destined to be repeated. There are days struggling with bureaucracy where individual officials are proven over and over to be caring but the system has managed to end up being uncaring in itself. There are hospitals where the chronically ill homeless wait with everyone else in Casualty but feel that the time spent is too long so they leave with infected wounds untreated, bronchitis undetected, and no preventive steps taken to ward off the illnesses that come with their way of life. Cheerfully and optimistically the book talks about curing scabies, getting medical cards, organising people to collect their social welfare, dealing with rat bites, fighting for more funds and for greater awareness.

The story of Trust, the organisation that has been a lifeline for so many people from so many backgrounds, is a heartening tale. It is not a story that will make you feel ashamed of your fellow citizens, because in general

Trust finds good people to help it fight its battles and to help people it has chosen to help. It is not a story that will make you feel impotently sad about the loneliness and loss in an unequal society; it is much more positive. It is not after your cheque book or your sense of guilty relief that you are not amongst the lost tonight. Instead it confirms the dignity of people and the diversity of ways that life can be lived. It offers no one total and permanent solution because homelessness is not just one kind of problem. In many cases it's not a problem at all, it's a choice.

And as always, those who do staggeringly generous work with all the hours of their day seem to have no idea how good they are. They have never wanted praise or recognition for themselves – just that the eyes and hearts of others be more open and less judgemental about their fellow countrymen and women who have chosen or have been directed by life to a different road from our own.

INTRODUCTION

WHY THIS BOOK?

There are some problems to which there are no solutions, some questions for which there are no easy answers. Life is about pain and happiness, joy and sorrow, and it is the mix and the balancing of these ingredients that gives it richness.

One of the reasons I am writing this book is to look at myself and encourage everyone else to do likewise. We need each other – and everyone, without exception, has a role and a value. My vision of life is that we are inter-dependent. Rich or poor, articulate or quiet, everyone has a part to play. One of the more questionable aspects of society today is the way that one section of the community is being made to feel useful and valuable while another section is being made to feel useless and worthless. This exclusion is unjust, unhealthy, and a great waste of human resources.

My basic mission is to share with a wider public the potential of the homeless people I work with. These are the people seen as failures by society. And yet some live happy and dignified lives. More could do so. Some of the factors preventing this arise from the perceptions and misconceptions of the public, of state, of institutions, as well as from the homeless people themselves.

The people I work with are often voiceless. Many have felt excluded from birth from making a contribution because of sad beginnings, personality difficulties, life experiences. Outwardly their appearance may be off-putting. They may look dirty, uncared-for, purposeless, perhaps dangerous. One of the aims of this book is to get behind that stereotyped view and examine why many homeless people present in this way. Looking well and smelling sweet is not simply a matter of soap, water and clean clothes. Many people with poor self-esteem feel there is no point in undertaking the daily task of looking clean and acceptable.

The point is that things are not always what they seem. Behind an obvious problem, there are deeper problems which take time, patience, commitment to work through; the application of some simple solution from a distance will simply not work.

I have no short-term answers to homelessness. Organis-ations that care, people who care, the provision of small-group home accommodation will help. But no matter how many units of accommodation we provide, there will always be people who feel excluded, who won't fit in. And this is because homelessness is a state of mind as well as a lack of shelter.

Homeless people need to be listened to and worked with patiently; they need respect, autonomy and space to live the lives they've chosen with minimum state inter-ference. As a society we need to accept that some people are different and will never conform. More long-term solutions involve changing hearts so that such people are not labelled or condemned but allowed to march to the beat of their own drum.

Who are our homeless people? A myth I would like to challenge is that they are all 'a problem'. Some are not. Some don't need or look for anything from society. I'm thinking of many who sleep rough, who do not want to be slotted into a graph or chart. Their days have their own rhythm and purpose. Our challenge is to accept their validity on their terms, rather than trying to change them to fit in with our idea of 'normal'.

Some homeless people do need and accept help. Sometimes with patience and sensitivity it is possible to become friends with them and offer in an acceptable way some services to improve their comfort and wellbeing. Sometimes it is not, and again, we must accept people's right to be different. We should think more of the complexity of the jigsaw and the importance of each individual piece.

Many homeless people live in hostels which become their homes. Some have psychological problems; some abuse alcohol and become violent. Others are gentle and quiet, no threat to themselves or anyone else. But generally speaking, the homeless population is a constantly changing tide. There are people who become homeless for short periods due to marital disharmony or family break-up. With the right approach, these new homeless poeple could be helped to overcome their difficulties. Often if someone is acting in a particular way, perhaps exhibiting anger or violence, this is a cover-up for feelings of hurt or rejection, or for a sense of injustice.

I would offer this challenge to some of the key people in organisations who work with homeless and poor people: 'Do I truly empathise with and respect the people I purport to represent?' It is my experience that people are drawn to this area of work for many reasons – some good and useful, others perhaps less so. There is a lot of power available to those who work for and apparently speak for 'the poor'.

Training should include the capacity to develop more empathy with the client, more challenge to the practitioner, rather than consist of the mere inculcation of a clinical set of standards and approaches. This leads on to the question of education. How we are educating children at primary and secondary, and young adults at third level? How are we supporting parents? How are we training people to live with one another? How are we training our professionals in the health and the caring services? How are we training people in the Church? How do we train the judiciary? Perhaps entry to some third-level courses should take as much account of the personality of the applicant as the number of points achieved in the Leaving Certificate.

I believe the way we label people is one of the problems of society today. Labels can be harmful and destructive. Labels can dehumanise and limit people, distance us from others and absolve us from the responsibility of mutual care. Vagrant, dosser, psycho, wino, gurrier, culchie, drop-out, pervert, the homeless – these are some of the labels attached to the people I work with, and yet I can offer no label, no umbrella term for them because they are just people, all different, with unique personalities and individual gifts, wounds and strengths.

If we label people it can free us from taking action on their behalf. It can limit their potential and their diversity. We can forget that someone without a permanent home could be a singer, a poet, a good worker, a gentle personality. He becomes 'the homeless'. He becomes the label and that is all we see. The language we use in talking about poverty is now as sophisticated as the language we use in medicine, in law. Language, like labels, can be a weapon of exclusion, making others feel deprived and ignored. Complicated jargon is a sign of our inability to be simple and, to my mind, simplicity is more powerful than sophistication. I have attended numerous poverty conferences where the jargon was so complex as to be inexplicable to the speakers, never mind the audience. People who have difficulty in expressing their feelings can hide behind the cloak of language.

Labelling and language are two steps to the tyranny of statistics which play a major role in the business of poverty. We are compiling so much information, conducting ever more surveys, asking so many questions; why then have things not changed for the better? I suggest that the wrong people are asking the wrong questions of the wrong people. I believe we need to listen more to homeless people themselves; we need to listen to some of the so-called powerless people who work with homeless people – home-helps, cleaners, porters, nurses – people on the ground without a lot of clout.

I don't think the answer is always to throw more money at a problem; in some ways that can be the easiest option. The more difficult and more effective approach is to explore new ways of being with people which can slowly lead to change and growth, ways that do not necessarily involve money. I remember Annie, whose cat was the most important thing in the world to her. It happened that Annie could no longer look after herself and she had to go to a hostel where no animals were allowed. The staff in that hostel were very good. They found a home for the cat, and one of them used to drive Annie out every week to visit the cat. These are the little things I'm talking about that don't cost money. Of course a more fundamental question could be asked: why not allow cats in the hostel? Many hostels are warm and comfortable but lack a feeling of home because they have no gardens, no growth, no animals, no feelings of being close to nature – the everyday touches that make a house a home.

Alice Leahy

1

A Day in the Life of Trust

In the 1970s I was a prisoner in Amsterdam on hunger strike (unsuccessful as it happened) against being extradited back to Ireland. I was released from prison in Ireland to my wife and family but with no preparation for readjustment to normal life.

A lot of family tensions followed. I left home, and arrived in Dublin with no money and a note for Simon with the recommendation that they give me a bed in exchange for work but they said I was too old.

Soon after, I found my way to Trust, and worked voluntarily for about two years. Then a vacancy for a full-time worker occurred and I was appointed. It has worked out very well, helping my personal as well as my working life. My family is united again and my youngest child is now at college.

Many homeless people my age have come from a somewhat similar background to my own, living in one room, existing on little money. Without any effort, I can understand how they feel. Equally, some young people regard going to gaol as a sign that they're Jack the Lad. I

*can tell them it's no big deal at all; crime doesn't pay; the
only people who benefit from petty crime are the solicitors and lawyers.*

*I constantly question the work we do. Are we really
helping anyone? I think one of the most valuable points is
that we exist, that the hostels know we exist, that homeless
people know we exist, and our very existence is a challenge
to everyone. However, when I answer the phone, because
I don't speak with a plum in my mouth, some people can't
leave the most simple of messages for me to pass on. I used
to find this irritating, until Alice pointed out that it's they
who have the problem, not me.*

Paddy Gallagher, Trust

Even before I reach work, I am at work. Often as I walk
in the early morning I meet Sean. He is in his sixties,
sleeps out all the time, drinks very heavily and spends
his day sitting in a small park with his bottle. I might meet
Tom who sleeps wrapped in a blanket under a tree by the
river bank. Tom has all his possessions in a plastic bag and
for a long time would not claim his allowance because he
could not cope with the red tape involved. We have now
arranged for Tom to collect his allowance from us each
week, and he is looking after himself a lot better as a result.
I might see Joe on his way to a food centre for breakfast.
Joe lives in a flat now but is still part of the homeless
network and uses a food centre for meals and friendship.

Often I call into the Meath Hospital in the early
morning. Many homeless people spend time in hospital
and our ongoing contact with hospital staff is very

important, particularly in organising discharge and aftercare. Robert was in hospital recently suffering from cardiac failure. His long-term drinking leads to leg ulcers. After discharge he would come to us to have his leg dressed but usually he drifts into neglect and the cycle begins again. I have told Robert that if he doesn't stop drinking he may lose his leg but he has no motivation to change. With others we are more successful in encouraging them to take more care of themselves.

Trust is in the basement of the Iveagh Hostel in Bride Road, Dublin. I arrive at about eight o'clock. My co-worker Paddy Gallagher will have been there since half past seven welcoming early callers and getting everything ready for the day. Paddy has been with us for twelve years and I sometimes feel that Trust could do without me but not without Paddy. Also, some homeless men don't like women and prefer to deal with Paddy.

Paddy Dunne and Noel Byrne are two full-time voluntary workers who live in the Iveagh Hostel. Noel cuts people's hair and does valuable maintenance work for us. Paddy accompanies people to hospital and in situations where they may feel confused or isolated on their own. Evelyn Magee, our voluntary secretary, comes in once a week, and our friend, Catherine Pearson, has a befriending role.

The homeless population is a shifting one and there are many degrees of homelessness. At the core are about forty people, mainly men, who sleep rough all the time. They can't or won't fit into a system they find alien, frightening or irrelevant. There are some hundreds of people who live in hostels, including long-stay residents for whom the hostel is their home. Many homeless people were reared in orphanages or were patients in psychiatric hospitals and may have personality or psychological problems.

There are people on the margins of homelessness due to temporary or long-term crisis. Some of these are in bed-and-breakfast accommodation. And there are women and children who escape from family violence to a Women's Aid hostel.

The homeless people with whom we have most contact sleep rough and have been homeless for a long time. They often bring new people to our notice. Many, but not all, abuse alcohol. We open the side gate at nine o'clock. Up to thirty people call each morning and no appointment is necessary.

Physically, Trust consists of a bathroom, washroom, toilets, sitting-room and office. But its heart is a large room, part reception, part store-room, part kitchen, which is the place where people put their heads round the door, see who's there, sit and have a cup of tea, or occasionally breakfast. Having a microwave means that those being offered a snack can have a better choice. We have no computers, no gadgetry, few rules and no labels.

There is no such thing as a typical morning. We may not see someone for months and he suddenly arrives. Others call regularly. Joe comes in often to wash his feet. Maureen may call for ointment. She lives in a women's hostel and is very nervous of men. She used to shout at the men when she first came to Trust. But she has grown fond of Noel and is more relaxed. She gives us exquisite Christmas cards every year, and her appreciation of fine things indicates that despite her appearance, Maureen is a cultured woman who, for some reason, has lost her way.

Mick may turn up out of the blue. He arrived recently with a black and swollen eye. He had been given a prescription for eye-drops at a hospital out-patient department but had no medical card and could not afford to pay. We had the prescription filled by a local chemist.

Marese may visit. A shy, reserved woman, she sleeps out winter and summer, and for many years lived in a cardboard box opposite Leinster House. She recently moved to a different street. Last summer Marese flew to London for her holidays and spent three weeks 'skippering' there before arriving home by boat. (A skipper is a place where people sleep rough; it may be an old car, a shed or under a tree or a canal bridge.) Now she is back in her doorway: independent, courteous, quiet – until she leaves again.

Many people contact us for basic needs such as washing, shaving, nail-cutting. Lice, scabies, cuts, bruises and skin ulcers are common. Being with someone during treatment often provides a vital human contact. At any one time we could have people waiting to choose clothes, receive medication, tonics, diet supplements or have a bath. We ask people to clean up after them – in many places nothing is expected of homeless people but we don't agree with that. We may refer someone to AA, and we often talk to young homeless people about the responsibilities involved in parenting. How we in Trust present ourselves is very important. Some of the people we work with can be angry and some mornings there may be potentially tense situations between callers which we have to diffuse.

Along the first wall of our main room we have clothes on hangers with shoes underneath. A good pair of shoes can make the difference between hospitalisation and survival within the homeless community. But someone living on less than £60 a week, paying £45 a week for a hostel, will find it impossible to save up for new shoes. We encourage people to have their shoes soled and their clothes cleaned. Some of the men are very fastidious. Tony, who slept rough, came in often for needle and thread and to iron his clothes. Sadly, he died in tragic circumstances in 1994.

Along the second wall we have a worktop with open shelving above holding basic medicines – ointments and skin preparations. We don't keep drugs or antibiotics. Another wall has the fridge, washing-machine and wash-basin. The final wall has a closed section for dressings and bandages, and an office corner with telephone. Finally there is the spot just inside the door where Paddy stands to welcome all callers.

The walls in Trust are decorated with prints and paint-ings, some the work of Paddy Gallagher. We have a bronze head of John McCarthy who slept rough in Fairview and was very well looked after by the local people. His funeral attracted a large congregation. John's head was used as a model for Jesus in a Stations of the Cross, and the sculpture was presented to us by Bishop Desmond Williams.

Crises occur. The day that Noel was found drowned in the Liffey was a signal for his friends to arrive sadden-ed and bewildered. I notice that many people gravitate to us in times of tragedy because we offer a sense of family and community. During a time of disruption in the Iveagh Hostel, one resident came down once a week and washed his hands. He never spoke. In a changing world he needed to know we were there.

During the morning we have visits and phone calls from hostel and hospital staff. We have a number of professionals who give their time voluntarily in general medical, nursing, psychiatric, legal, dental and financial areas. A psychiatric nurse from St Brendan's Hospital calls regularly. A chiropodist calls once a month. A local doctor, John Latham, sometimes calls in on his way to work. Many people have serious undiagnosed illnesses or chronic conditions and we often refer them to hospital.

We are in regular contact with the main city hostels: the *Regina Coeli*, Morning Star, Model Lodging House, the St Vincent de Paul hostel in Back Lane, Simon, the Salvation Army hostel in Granby Row and their shelter in the grounds of St Brendan's Hospital. Some Wednesdays we visit the hostels. Often quite small issues can cause disproportionate reactions because of the sense of insecurity and high degree of dependency among hostel dwellers. Every Thursday morning there is a special session for Iveagh Hostel residents in Trust, offering a day-hospital facility and encouraging socialisation. Also on Thursday we have begun a day-care programme for a long-term prisoner pre-release.

At noon we close our side gate and spend some time reflecting on the morning's work. We feel such discussion is important if we are to offer an honest, non-judgemental yet challenging service to the people we work with. We don't pry. We convey empathy and concern. Our philosophy is to help people to look at the circumstances of their lives when they are ready. It is not always possible to make sense of the past or to allocate blame. Generally we encourage people to get on with their lives from this day forward and we believe it is never to late to start again.

Some of the afternoon is spent in administration. We may contact hostel staffs and others in related agencies, make appointments, follow up enquiries. We regularly receive calls from family members trying to trace or keep in touch with a homeless relative.

During the afternoon I may see by arrangement a homeless person for a cup of coffee. I may have to identify a body at the morgue. I may be visiting someone in prison or at Our Lady's Hospice, Harold's Cross. At night I may be addressing a group of nurses or business people on issues of homelessness. Students on projects often contact us, wanting instant answers to complex questions such as: 'How do people become homeless?'; 'What do they look like?'. We have an educational role in explaining the needs of homeless people to a wide range of professionals including medical and nursing students, religious or community groups and media. We occasionally have people on placement with us.

I serve on a number of committees and there may be meetings early morning or late at night. Occasionally I accompany the Simon outreach worker at night to meet people sleeping rough.

Every day is different. All of them are fairly exhausting. I suppose what we give most to each person is time. A day in which we see only three people can be as rewarding and as important as a day in which we see thirty-three. Every day gives the opportunity and the choice to make a difference.

2
—

EARLY DAYS – ALICE

From my experience in caring organisations, it is clear that many homeless people have had a background of misfortune and hardship. This has psychologically damaged them in separating them from what is called normal society. Many come from broken families, may never have had the normal parental love and support during childhood and adolescence to develop in a stable manner.

We do not give sufficient attention to the psychological welfare of our children. While there is now awareness of the damaging consequences of physical and sexual abuse, there are less obvious types of parental abuse and neglect. Far too many parents damage their children by a lack of love and understanding and so set them on the road to an unhappy adulthood. In extreme cases, this leads to long-term psychiatric care, alcohol dependence, a street doorway or a hostel.

We need more education for parenting directed at parents and at school pupils, so that when they become parents, they will be more aware of the sensitivity and vulnerability of their children. This may not be the only answer to the problems of homelessness but it will go a long way towards reducing the numbers who descend to this unhappy existence.

Joseph Robins, former Assistant Secretary to the Department of Health

I was born in Fethard, County Tipperary on the Annsgift estate, a 400-acre mixed dairy and tillage farm then owned by the Hughes family. Four generations of my father's family have now worked on Annsgift. When I was born my grandfather was the family steward, my father duly succeeding him. His first wages were ten shillings (50p) a week, including a house. Two of my brothers still work on the farm, although its ownership has changed and its produce widened to include flowers for export.

I was born at home in 1942. We were a family of three boys and two girls. My father loved his work and was close to nature. A secure, happy man, he had the kind of wisdom that doesn't come from books. I remember once getting into a sulk because I was going to a film, *Seven Little Foys*, and wanted to sit in the balcony but could only afford the pit. My father said, 'You'll see exactly the same film from the pit as from the balcony.' I've never forgotten it. Your vantage point may be less important than your vision.

My father loved animals and I grew up accustomed to sick animals being nursed by the fire. He died in 1992 and up to the day he went to hospital he was still personally caring for the animals. We were all involved in the work of the farm, up at 4 am on fair day helping to feed the animals and get them ready.

My mother is Hannie Crean. Her family were small farmers nearby. She was and is a strong contented woman and a great provider. She was always washing, knitting, mending, cooking, baking, letter-writing and reading. My parents were into role-sharing naturally. My father dug the vegetables needed for dinner each day, brought in firewood, polished his own shoes.

In fact, we all had a role and a value which taught me a lot. Work was an important part of my upbringing in the sense of always being usefully occupied. We were an interdependent community and through everyone's efforts it worked. We didn't have a lot of money but I never felt poor. I used to think I came from a typical family but I now know I was privileged. While I got my core values from my parents, being part of the extended Hughes family gave us a unique breadth and vision.

We lived only a few minutes away from the Big House by a short cut. Although Protestant, Major Hughes lent us the green van to drive to Mass each Sunday. We had Christmas dinner with the family every year. There was a mutual respect, not a master–servant relationship. Because I met no class distinction I am able to treat everyone the same and feel absolutely comfortable in all situations.

We were a resourceful family. Everything was recycled. We grew vegetables, fertilised by farmyard manure from the Big House. We gathered nettles and berries and made soup, jams and chutneys. We baked bread. Our hens provided eggs, and we helped Mrs Hughes preserve these in waterglass for when the hens were not laying. The cows gave milk and butter. We cured sheepskins for rugs, and one of my jobs was to collect sheep wool from the ditches.

I spent hours sifting, carding and spinning this into wool for lumra rugs. The Hugheses kept bees and sold honey.

Absolutely nothing was wasted. The feathers of our Christmas goose went to stuff our home-made pillows. Flour bags provided the pillow covers. Canvas bags which had once held dry goods were embroidered and used for cushions. Cold tea-leaves were sprinkled on the stone kitchen floor to keep down the dust. Sheep droppings and rain water guaranteed my grandmother lovely geraniums.

I remember we had no electricity and no running water at first. Both came later. We cooked and baked over the big open fire and drew water from the well. Hams were smoked as they hung from the high ceiling. In the autumn we picked chestnuts and roasted them in the hot ashes.

We never had a doctor. When once I broke my nose I went to the local bone-setter, Mrs Walsh, my mother's aunt, the visit ending, as all consultations did, with tea and home-made scones. Every day we had a calcium tablet and a spoonful of cod-liver oil and malt. We drank buttermilk and rubbed a raw potato on chilblains during winter. (There was a downside to a simpler health service. My teeth were crossed over and instead of correcting this, the school dentist pulled them all out.)

I wore home-knitted jumpers and some of my clothes were secondhand, which I didn't like. Clothes were mended and darned rather than consigned to the bin. The daily newspaper was shared between a number of families and we read the *National Geographic* magazine which the Hugheses ordered on subscription. We made our own amusement. My grandfather conducted question time round the fire, and used the flickering shadows to conjure with his hands animal shapes which we had to identify. We played with jigsaws and paints; we had a gramophone and a wireless. We got books from the library and the Hugheses gave us nature books and atlases.

There was a lot of emphasis on getting involved. We children wrote to newspapers, entered competitions, wrote stories and poems. There was a high element of volunteerism though nobody called it that. We use to clean local graveyards and visit elderly people in the old county home in Cashel. I grew up with a strong feeling that everyone was important. Once a month the Delaneys, a travelling family, came to town and always visited my grandfather. They would chat about the weather, their travels, and they might sell some of their craftwork – or might not. If they didn't appear, somehow people missed them and hoped all was well.

We had a drama group in Fethard and Mrs Hughes sometimes took us to opera in Clonmel. We also had the fit-up. A travelling company put on plays at the crossroads near our house every year. We had dancing at the crossroads in summer evenings, on a wooden platform built under the trees.

In the summer too I remember bringing tea, gallons of it, and sandwiches to the workers in the fields. There was the sound of birdsong, the smell of new-mown grass. In my childhood memories there is a great abundance of wildlife. (Where are all the frogs gone?) I spent a lot of time sitting by the stream daydreaming, and the memories now are of space and peace.

We were enthusiastic sports followers. My father was a member of Coolmoyle hurling club, and it was nothing to cycle twelve miles to support our team. In summer too we were paid to pick fruit for Mrs Hughes, working a proper day with an hour off for lunch.

Olivia Hughes with Muriel Gahan founded Country Markets in 1947 to develop rural communities through selling produce and crafts. The first branch was founded in Fethard by my mother and Mrs Hughes, who also co-founded the local Irish Countrywomen's Association guild. My mother was treasurer and secretary of Country Markets, a post she held for thirty-one years. The two women had a great respect for each other. With no children of her own, Olivia Hughes took a great interest in us. When we began a junior branch of Macra na Tuaithe she gave us the house annexe for meetings. We were a properly constituted branch with secretary, chair and treasurer; we met each month, held debates and had guest speakers.

A hallmark of Macra is the doing of projects. Mine was a guinea-pig breeding project which was very important to me in my teens. Major Hughes got me six guinea pigs. I made a hutch for them in the orchard and it was my job to keep them fed, watered, clean and healthy. Though the Hugheses, I made contact with the laboratory at Trinity College Dublin, which used guinea pigs for research.

Every few weeks I would load my guinea pigs into special boxes, strap them to my bicycle and cycle three miles to Fethard station, put them on the train to Dublin and telegraph Trinity so that they would be met at the other end. At one stage I had sixty guinea pigs. The project won me the runner-up Young Farmer of the Year award in South Tipperary. Eventually I lost some guinea pigs to the foxes, Trinity's need lessened and the project came to a natural end.

But I had learned a lot. I had learned about responsibility, reliability, keeping accounts and records.

When I was growing up, religion was seen as rules and regulations, prayers at set times like the Angelus, grace before meals, the family Rosary, May processions, the parish mission with the Redemptorists thundering from the pulpit. However, I didn't see the church as an oppressive or particularly important force, just another part of the community. My own religious beliefs would have been nurtured by my daily environment.

Like others before me I walked to school through the fields. We used to collect wood for the classroom fire in primary school. When I went to the Presentation Convent in Fethard I became conscious of class difference. I sensed a tremendous snobbery. Only those who could afford to did music and tennis. I came to see as I got older that social life was based on property. I remember being at a local farmers' meeting and being told, 'This meeting is only for farmers', which infuriated me.

I loved animals and wanted to be a vet when I left school but there wasn't the money to train me. Nursing too seemed out of the question due to the training fees asked by some hospitals. But the Hughes family backed my application to the Royal City of Dublin Hospital, Baggot Street. I was accepted, and to help earn my fees I got a summer job as a chambermaid in the Ormond Hotel in Clonmel, now gone. I remember the people who impressed me most were the cleaning staff.

3

EARLY DAYS – PAUL

I was born in Dublin in 1950 in a large three-storey house owned by my father. We lived in the basement and had two upstairs rooms also. My mother's sister, Joan, had her own flat in the house. My brother Daniel was three years older than me and when I was eight my mother adopted a baby girl, Lillian, whose mother had died in childbirth. Lillian's father was our lodger. When I was eleven my mother had another child, my sister Eileen.

My father was a bricklayer. I think he was given the house by his father but I'm not sure. My mother was always very busy looking after us all. There was a lot of work to do. I remember she used to be in a bad humour on Monday, which was washday. She washed the clothes by hand and scrubbed shirt collars and cuffs on a wooden board.

I was very close to my mother. Everyone liked her. She was kind and loving, and had a great sense of humour. My relationship with my father was very different. Frankly I was frightened of him. He was distant and silent, and

the only time he spoke was to issue orders and instruct-
ions. He was football-mad and used to drag me off to local
football matches. I dreaded it, sitting in old buildings in
the cold. I had no interest in sport and went for his sake
but mainly I remember the fear I had of him and the
feeling that no matter what I did, I could not please him.

My father worshipped Daniel and I didn't think he
cared for me. I didn't mind because it kept him out of
my way except when he noticed I liked reading and would
give out to my mother, 'What's he doing with his head
stuck in a book. That's no use to him.'

There is one night that is still etched deeply in my
mind. My parents had gone out so Daniel and I climbed
down the drainpipe and went off to explore. But someone
saw us and told my father. When we came home he was
waiting for us. He locked the bedroom door, stripped us
both naked and beat us with his belt. I was about seven
at the time and cried my eyes out but Daniel never said
a word. I hated my father after that. I had been slapped
before but it paled into insignificance compared to this.
My mother was downstairs, very distressed, but not
allowed to interfere. I think she was frightened of my
father but I don't believe he was violent towards her. One
night she told me to get up, got me dressed and we hid
in the coal-shed. We heard my father coming home, going
up to bed and later when all was quiet, she put me back
to bed. I didn't know what that was about, I still don't. I
believe my mother and father did love each other and I
have vague memories of tenderness between them.

My father had good qualities. We never went hungry.
He would have killed anyone who touched my mother. I

later came to know and understand him a bit more. He was the eldest of thirteen children and never had a proper childhood. His father had a coal business, and by age ten my father was heaving coal on his back before he went to school. His mother was very tough and I don't think he had much love growing up.

My relationship with Daniel was complex. I hero-worshipped him but also resented him for being pre-ferred. I didn't have much time for my sisters, whom I regarded as bloody nuisances. My aunt Joan had married and took over the ground floor in our house. I was very fond of her husband Jimmy and was able to talk to him about lots of things. He grew to be more of a father-figure for me than my own father.

As a child I tended to be quiet and thoughtful. I used to creep out on the flat roof at night to look at the stars. One night they couldn't find me in my bed and started a big search. I was on the roof all the time. Sometimes I wet the bed. I don't know why.

I went to the local primary school. At school I palled with another boy, Michael, who was also very good and quiet. He used to come home and help his mother every day after school and I got into the habit of doing the same. My mother was delighted. But then for some reason I had to go to the doctor and I remember sitting in the waiting room and hearing the doctor say, 'What are you giving this boy; he's starving!' Apparently I was suffering from pernicious anaemia. For months before that I had found a way of not eating food I disliked. It was a tip I had picked up on the radio serial *The Archers*. I came to dinner with an old newspaper on my lap and during the meal I used to slide pieces of meat and vegetables unnoticed off my plate to the newspaper. Later I'd roll up the paper and throw it in the bin. I had been living on bread and jam for ages, and had obviously no energy to be other than well behaved!

Once my condition was diagnosed, I was admitted to the Children's Hospital, Temple Street, to have pints of blood pumped into me, and get built up. I was there for six weeks. When I came out of hospital I dropped Michael like a shot and got in with a gang, began robbing orchards and generally behaving like a young healthy lad.

Looking back I feel I had quite a happy childhood except for one thing. When I was about seven, Daniel started sexually abusing me. He would have been about ten and I learnt later he had been sexually abused by a stranger, which may have started this behaviour. I was bewildered, and what he did hurt me and made me feel very uncomfortable. He warned me to tell nobody and threatened me with all kinds of consequences if I ever spoke. I didn't dare speak, but one morning at breakfast I terrified him by telling my mother that I dreamt the bed was a rocking boat. She didn't know what I was talking about but he did, and he laid off me for a while.

The abuse went on for some years, ending only when Daniel got a girlfriend. The abuse changed my relationship with him. I tried to avoid him as much as possible. There was nobody I could talk to about it, and I suppose I dealt with it by trying to put it out of my mind. But it cast a very long shadow and had repercussions for years.

4

MOVING TO DUBLIN – ALICE

Nurses are the only professional group trained exclusively within the health service. Most student nurses enter straight from school into a hierarchical training system. To survive, they rapidly learn to conform. Hospital research in the 1980s found that student nurses' experiences encouraged adaptation to the system, an adaptation seldom reflected on and usually internalised by the end of training.

Most nurses are women. It has been argued that, out of mistaken loyalty, women often support structures and practices which are oppressive to others. Alternatively, the internalisation may have been refined to the extent that nurses have ceased to see injustice and have identified with the oppressive system. Anyone who demonstrates against this may provoke a storm of protest, as happened when research showed that some patients are treated differently if they are unpopular with nurses.

Rebels, whether patients or staff, have a hard time in hospitals. Many nurses who maintain a rebellious steak leave the hospital system and exercise their caring role to great effect in a different environment.

Judith Chavasse, former director of the Department of Nursing, University College, Dublin

The first major upheaval in my life was moving to Dublin to train as a nurse in Baggot Street Hospital. I was eighteen and it was 1961. That first evening in the nurses' home I had toad-in-the-hole, the first time I tasted it, all part of the new adventure. There was a lovely open fire in the sitting-room and I felt welcome.

From the beginning, we trainees were very aware of our junior status. In the sitting-room, senior nurses sat by the fire and would look at you if you sat in 'their' seats, so you had to move out to the colder edges. Soon we realised that the hospital uniform was very cumbersome. The black stockings were thick, the shoes heavy, the blue dresses with starched apron, collar and hat were stiff and difficult to work in.

Burden or not, the uniform carried with it a spurious sense of power and status. People asked my advice. Two months up from the country, I was incorrectly regarded as an authority. Uniform, a dress code, ceremonial trappings are often used to create an elite that can alienate and disempower the public.

At the end of May I received my first pay cheque – £2/9s/7d. (£2.48), which included board and lodging. We had one day a month off and needed permission from matron to be out after 9 pm. I was getting to know Dublin, finding my way to the National Gallery, National Museum, National

Library, browsing around old statues and monuments, the cafés and dance halls. In some ways I was beginning to re-create in Dublin the life I had in Fethard.

In June 1961 I recorded my first blood pressure, prepared my first appendix for theatre and did my first enema with soap and water, funnel and tube. I had experienced my first hospital death and a suicide attempt by a patient. I was learning to respect patients' confidences and be a good listener. I went to lectures at the College of Surgeons as part of first-year theory. In June I moved to the large dormitory in the nurses' home, a long low-ceilinged room with no privacy. In the years since, working with people who live in hostel dormitory accommodation, I can empathise with their difficulty. Living like this, there is no place to undress in privacy, no place to reflect, no place just to be. In our dormitory a set of curtains round each bed would have been an improvement but this was never considered.

On 1 July, I gave my first injection. In the autumn I joined An Óige, (annual membership ten shillings [50p]) and the Ballsbridge library, and continued to explore the many features of a capital city.

One new experience that year was night duty, which included cooking for senior staff. Night sisters' meals were a particular ordeal. We wrestled with large industrial cookers and carried the cooked food on trays down to personnel on various floors. Frequently our efforts were unappreciated and there were many unkind and cutting, though probably accurate, comments.

While we received a very structured and strict medical training, there was a blurring of our domestic and our medical roles in the first year. We were cheap labour. We did work now done by cleaning staff: cleaning wards, bathrooms and toilets. We cleaned, set and lit the fires in the wards each morning. We set the breakfast trays and did the washing-up after some meals.

We spent endless hours at a long wooden table in the middle of a large ward rolling cotton wool into balls and putting them into containers to be autoclaved, (sterilised). There was also a sewing-room, where women darned and mended bedlinen, towels, curtains and clothing. While all this work was labour intensive, it had an ethos of harnessing resources, of being frugal and prudent with equipment. Today we save money on laundry and labour by opting for disposable sheets, syringes, dressings and other equipment. But using something once and throwing it out goes against the grain with me – and has added to unemployment.

The poet, Patrick Kavanagh, was one of my patients in 1961. Brendan Behan was an occasional patient also but the two men did not get on well together. Patrick Kavanagh seemed sad, morose, while Brendan Behan was very different – generous, outgoing, warm.

One diary entry for December records that a patient spent sixteen hours in theatre. The year ended on a sad note for one family. On 28 December a sixteen-year-old boy was admitted, dead on arrival, the victim of a road traffic accident.

In spring 1962 a new student group came on stream. We were no longer the juniors and had begun our slow creep up the ladder. We began lectures in domestic science and food hygiene at the College of Catering,

Cathal Brugha Street, and learnt invalid cooking, egg-nogs, steamed fish, carrigeen mould, as we were expected occasionally to cook for patients.

Socially I was finding my feet. I joined the ICA. I enrolled in the German Institute to learn German. Classes were held once a week; the cost, twenty-five shillings (£1.25) per term.

Hospital life has a very hierarchical structure. At the top are consultants, medical personnel, senior nursing staff; then down to nurses, domestic staff, porters and cleaners. From the beginning I found myself often drawn to domestic staff and cleaners at the bottom of the pile. During 1962 I worked in the out-patients department. I remember admitting one man who had drunk a whole bottle of 4711 perfume. Years later in Simon I dealt with a similar incident when a woman alcoholic drank a bottle of the same perfume.

Then as now people come by appointment to out-patients. The system of booking dozens of people at the same time for an out-patient appointment is appalling. It should be possible and it would certainly be more efficient and more caring to stagger appointments during the day. The system indicates the relative values we ascribe to different categories of people. It is saying that the consultant can't be kept waiting for one second but that so-called ordinary people are expected to wait for hours, often with small children, and at great inconvenience.

My monthly pay cheque in March 1962 was £12/9s/8d (£12.85). Later that year I was transferred to the cardiac unit, a big responsibility. A diary entry after a night-duty shift on my own from 1 am to 4.30 am reads:

'Thank God, everything was OK.'

In 1963 we did our surgery examination in the College of Surgeons. I came third, beaten for second place by one mark. I began new German classes and a dress-designing course and donated my first pint of blood at Pelican House. Gradually as 1963 progressed a new kind of entry crept into my diary. I wrote, 'I feel lonely and tired.' Often we came off duty and were too tired to do anything other than sleep, although we were often expected to attend lectures and classes on our day off. I got a tonic which helped a bit. I decided to discontinue the German classes until May. I was feeling the pressure of non-stop work.

Also as nurses our point of view was often ignored. One day a few other nurses and I decided to complain to matron about the quality of the patients' food. We had arranged to meet outside her door early one morning. Nobody else turned up so I went in on my own and I said my piece. Her response was: 'What would your mother say if she heard all this?' I regarded it as a kind of emotional blackmail, with no notice taken of the points made.

On 22 November 1963 we were in the sitting-room of the nurses' home when we learnt that the American president, John Kennedy, had been assassinated in Dallas. The atmosphere was of sudden tragedy and doom. We all felt it keenly, young and hopeful as we were.

At 2.30 am one cold morning in January 1964 I sat in the window and wrote eight pages, describing my life since I started nursing. I decided to write a book (a goal that was to take three decades to achieve). Two months later Brendan Behan died in the Meath Hospital. Later that year I had my first contact with St Brendan's Psychiatric

Hospital, accompanying a member of staff there. Little did I know then that a large part of my future life would be among people who knew psychiatric hospitals too well.

I bought a bicycle in 1964 for £7/10s. (£7.50) and used it extensively for trips to the sea and the country. Our final exams were in May that year. Cycling furiously to Bray and Killiney kept me sane during stressful examination times.

9 February 1965: our last day as a group of student nurses together. They had been four good years. We had made our own community. We sat that night playing records. We had grown close and realised that one chapter of our lives was drawing to a end.

One major reservation about my training was that it lacked any real discussion about the social aspects of the disease and the links between health and lifestyle. The structured lectures were too theoretical, with little application to real people in real-life situations.

Once I qualified, I had decided to do a midwifery course and had been accepted by the Rotunda Hospital. I went home for six weeks and worked in the county home, St Patrick's Hospital, the place I had often visited as a young girl. I loved every minute of my time there. There was a great feeling of mutual care, concern and warmth. The patients were on first-name terms with each other and with staff. There was no distinction made between the domestic staff, nurses, porters and nuns. Everyone shared a common agenda: to work together for the mutual good.

In April 1965 I came back to Dublin. ('I hate coming to Dublin again,' I wrote in my diary) and the Rotunda.

Soon I was assigned to the labour ward. I remember my first time doing a rectal examination and feeling the baby. It was a breech birth and the first thing I felt were the tiny toes. It was a boy weighing 9lb 5oz. His mother was from the Gardiner Street flats nearby; he was the fifth in the family, and his mother called him Paul.

I found some midwifery lectures very interesting. The role of the social worker was vital to many patients with social problems. Looking back now I realise our attitude to stillborn babies was very thoughtless: the child was taken from the mother, who was often put back in the post-natal ward with the other mothers. Some women who gave birth to handicapped children were treated insensitively also. There was little thought given to the sense of loss experienced and the adjustment needed for parents who had anything other than perfect birth.

One night in March 1966 I had been to a dance in Clery's and was home at 2.30 am, when I heard a muffled roar. It was Nelson's Pillar being blown up. Another landmark gone, this time very dramatically.

At that time the hospital still had a district service. Midwives delivered mothers of babies at home. I remember going out in the middle of the night with the sister-in-charge. Some of the people we visited were very poor. Whole families lived in one room. You are challenged on how you operate as a nurse outside the clinical setting. At the end of the year I did well in my oral and written examinations.

I spent 1966 working as a staff nurse on the pre-natal ward and while I enjoyed it, I was constantly struck by the terrible lack of privacy accorded to the patients. I return to the issue of space. They had so little personal space in the public wards, particularly in comparison to the private facilities. I would say the medical care was equally good in both but there was more space in the private wards, more colour, better food, presented more attractively, and a lot of little extras not on offer in the public wards. In the semi-private wards there were curtains around the beds.

I was also aware of the relative powerlessness of the patient and the power of the consultant and his entourage. The bevy of white-coated professionals who swung through the hospital on their rounds every day regarded women as their territory. Women had their abdomens felt, the foetal hearts listened to, their symptoms catalogued. Women were discussed and dissected as if they were not there.

The women themselves were great. Coming in to have the baby was their annual holiday. Many of them were very open about their sad lives and many husbands too did their best in obviously difficult circumstances. I met two women recently whom I had nursed in childbirth. In one case, the daughter in question is now a politician in the north city. The other mother's son ended his life in the Liffey.

5
—

TRAGEDY – PAUL

*The Department of Health started preparing new childcare
legislation in 1974. It came on the statute books in 1991.
Even in 1995, we hold our breath as less than a quarter
has been implemented.*

*One of the greatest challenges facing us in Ireland
today is to help the growing number of young people aged
between twelve and eighteen who cannot stay in their own
homes. Most come from neighbourhoods with levels of
unemployment and poverty which would have been un-
thinkable twenty years ago, where whole communities
have fallen apart through lack of facilities, and are now
being destroyed by drugs and violence. These young people
who are out of home in Irish cities are being exploited
socially, emotionally, physically and sexually – and their
numbers have increased tenfold since I started work in the
mid-eighties.*

*Youth homelessness is neither accidental nor excusable.
The blame lies squarely with our policy-makers and with
you and me. We have unthinkingly and readily created and
supported policies and procedures which have led to the*

46

*intolerable situation of these children and young people.
There is still time to turn from our indifference and to call
loudly and clearly for justice, love and action, to develop
services and policies which will help prevent, alleviate and
work towards the elimination of youth homelessness at all
levels.*

*Sister Stanislaus Kennedy, founder of Focus Point, now
director of Focus Ireland, the organisation's research and
educational arm*

My childhood ended when I started in the secondary
classes at the local religious-run school. The very first day
I fell foul of a tall, burly thug masquerading as a teacher
who picked me out for special treatment. I hadn't been
looking forward to big school anyway. A few years earlier
Daniel come home with his hands swollen to twice their
size from a lashing. I regarded school as a place of
incarceration.

We had this teacher for Irish, Maths and Religion. He
was universally detested; he bullied many boys but me
in particular. 'You'll never be as good as your brother,'
he would say, using the leather strap for emphasis. The
punishments became a self-fulfilling prophecy. I was so
afraid of being beaten that whenever he asked me a
question I would lose my train of thought, freeze and so
get beaten again.

I told my parents. They were sympathetic but felt I had
to manage as best as I could. But one day I couldn't take
it any more and I ran away from home. Another boy and
I drew money out of our post-office accounts and bought

a tent and tinned food. (I left in a shilling which kept the account open.) We took a bus up to the Dublin mountains, put up the tent but discovered we had no tin opener, and became cold, frightened and hungry in the dark. In the middle of the night we took down the tent and began to walk home. (I wonder what lucky person found the hoard of tinned food!) We arrived in our street at five o'clock in the morning. I didn't go home, but fell asleep on a windowsill in a neighbour's house. Later she woke me and told me my parents had been to the gardai and were looking for us everywhere. They were so relieved to see me that I wasn't punished, and they said I needn't go back to school.

I hadn't a clue what I wanted to do. I was too young to be apprenticed to a trade. My Uncle Jimmy didn't want me to leave school. He told me an education was an important thing and I would regret it later if I left now. But I didn't listen, didn't understand then. My first job was a messenger-boy for a gentlemen's outfitters. I had a bike; it was the summertime; and I loved riding around town, delivering parcels and letters and running messages.

The job lasted a few months. It ended when I mixed up the addresses on two parcels. The people phoned and complained and my boss gave out to me. My response was: 'You can keep your job.' I walked out. Now much later, I realise I ran away from him because I was afraid of his anger. I couldn't handle conflict. If I sensed someone was going to be angry with me, I would get in first and walk away. This began to be a pattern.

I found my next job myself at a local cinema. It entailed reporting for work in the morning to sweep and

clean the cinema, coming back for the afternoon perform-
ance and then again for the night show. I got £5 a week.
That first week my mother put the fiver on the shelf for
my father to see and be proud of me. I gave her £3 a week
and kept £2. My share went mainly on hire-purchase
repayments for my own bike.

The job was all right and I got to see a lot of films. I
hated war films, having a recurrent nightmare during my
childhood in which a bomb had been dropped, everyone
was screaming and crying and I was lost. I remember an
arm sticking up from the rubble. So I wasn't pleased when
The Longest Day came to the cinema, and was disgusted
to learn it was retained a second week 'by popular
demand'. It became my longest week.

At this stage I saw very little of my father. Our hours
didn't coincide and that suited me fine. I didn't miss
school at all and liked the people I worked with. We had
moved to a smaller house with no more lodgers which
delighted my mother. An Irish building strike meant my
father went to England to find work. He sent money home
regularly. I remember coming home and watching television with my mother, just the two of us. That was a
good time.

My mother died when I was fifteen and my life changed
for ever. She had suffered from asthma and high blood
pressure and was in hospital for some tests. She had been
getting better and was due home one Saturday. I had
visited her every day and was looking forward to having
her home. Cycling from work on the Friday night, I got
some premonition of disaster and instead of going home,
I went to my aunt and uncle. The babysitter came down

the stairs crying her eyes out, then Aunt Joan walked out of the sitting-room and I realised something was very wrong. My mother had died of a massive brain haemorrhage. When it began to sink in, I went berserk and was inconsolable.

The next day I saw my mother in the hospital morgue. She was lying on a slab, her head was bandaged and when I held her hand it too felt like marble. She was thirty-nine when she died. She was warm-hearted and lively and people loved her.

The funeral was terrible. My father was devastated but being my father, he showed nothing. Immediately after the funeral, Daniel packed up without a word and went to England. The night before we had shared a room together for the first time in ages and this time it was I who asked could I get into bed with him; it was I who made the sexual advances. I don't think I knew what I was doing. I was totally confused, looking for some kind of love and comfort.

My feelings at this time were indescribable. Everyone loved my mother but I feel I was especially close to her. I couldn't talk to anyone. Then to make matters worse, we had to go and live with my father in his parents' house in another part of the city. I knew instinctively the move was a bad idea.

I had always disliked my grandmother but now I came to hate her. She made us call her 'Nana', a title I detest. She was unkind, snobbish and small-minded. She insisted my grandfather eat on his own in the kitchen. She told me that years earlier she had made him move out of her room. She said she married him for his money but he had drunk it all and she never forgave him. She had ruled her own children with an iron hand and they moved away as soon as possible when they grew up. She singled one son out for the church and was disgusted when he didn't stay. Later, she refused to go to his wedding and was heard to remark that not only did he leave the priesthood, but he had the cheek to marry a hairdresser from Drimnagh!

There was one daughter, Nora, left at home. She was tough like her mother. My grandfather never had a good word to say about his wife or daughter, whom he called 'the henchwomen'. He was a nice man, though looking back I suppose he must have been weak to allow his wife to damage the family so much.

Basically the two women gave us a hard time. My two young sisters, then aged seven and four, were bewildered and insecure at the death of my mother but received very little love or affection. At the weekend my grandmother had them up early to clean the house from top to bottom. Next I found she was discriminating against Lillian, my adopted sister. One day I came home to find Lillian crying and learnt that Nora had told Lillian of her adoption. From then on I began to be particularly protective of my adopted sister.

Unfortunately my father also began to discriminate against her. It was a terrible time. I was out of my mind with confusion and grief. I had left my job in the cinema and was working on a building site. My grandmother obviously found me very difficult and one night in order to frighten me she sent me off to a hostel. I spent a night in the Morning Star Hostel, among men who were much older than me, some broken and alcoholic. It was a terrible experience. My grandmother said, 'That's where you'll end up sleeping unless you mend your ways,' which, with hindsight, was one of the few things she got right!

One day I came home to find my father on the phone to an aunt of his in England asking if I could come and live with them. He never said anything to me about it nor I to him, but I wasn't surprised a few weeks later when they came to Ireland for their annual holiday and took me out for a meal on my own.

I liked this couple. Their two sons had been killed in the war and they had been kind to us over the years. They asked me would I come back with them in Cheshire, and within three days I was packed and gone, almost without a backward glance. Lillian would have been the one reason to have kept me here but arrangements had already been made for her to return to her father who had since married and could offer her a home. I felt that even if I had stayed I wouldn't have been able to see much of her and, anyway, I was so crushed myself I couldn't think straight. Nothing was fitting in and I felt I was going out of my mind. My grandmother wanted to pin all kinds of medals to me as I was leaving. She described England as a 'cesspool of sin' but I think she was glad to get rid of me all the same. I had no particular feelings about leaving my young sister Eileen and I never said goodbye to my father. By now I couldn't stand the sight of him and he knew it.

In Cheshire I got a job as a waiter in a local hotel. My aunt and uncle did their best but I was very unhappy. Nothing made sense. I was very angry and mixed up about my mother's death and there was nobody to talk to about it. I had my sixteenth birthday and soon another problem emerged. I began to find myself attracted to men rather than to women. I was very frightened of these feelings and did not know how to deal with them. After eighteen months in England I decided I must go home. I hoped I could leave these new feelings behind me. My aunt and uncle were upset at my leaving and it was difficult to give them a reason that they understood.

My father met me at Dublin Airport. We had had no contact for a long time and he realised the quiet boy had been replaced by an angry young man. I told him I wasn't going home but would be living with my aunt and uncle. I had feelings inside me that I could neither understand or control. I found it difficult to trust people. I had trusted my mother and she had gone. I felt that I could never get close to anyone again, because if I did, and they too were taken away, I would be worse off than before.

6

DISENCHANTMENT
EDGING INTO SOCIAL WORK – ALICE

Dublin has a long tradition of voluntary help for homeless people, ranging from homes to hostels to food and day centres. Also, Crosscare and the Conference of Religious in Ireland regularly include advocacy for the homeless in statements at budget time and in negotiations with health boards and local authorities.

Can we sit back and feel there is no more to be done? More is needed before we can claim to be living up to the standards of our gospel as a society and as individuals. 'The poor you shall always have with you,' should not lead us to be satisfied with a society that both creates and perpetuates poverty.

What can we do? We can involve ourselves in the many voluntary efforts to ease the burden of homeless people. We can treat them with the dignity that their humanity demands of us. We can support voluntary action and influence public bodies to act decisively in favour of the homeless people. We can pray that parish communties will come to realise that caring for the marginalised is akin to caring for Christ because of the Christ in each person we meet.

Bishop Desmond Williams on the role of the Church in combating homelessness

In 1967 Father Sean O'Neill who worked with the Pro-Cathedral adoption society, invited me to visit families who had adopted children and talk to them about baby-care. I also began visiting a children's home in Blackrock. The Rotunda social work department worked with home-less girls and in Dominic Street Friary, Father Feargal O'Connor was active in helping single pregnant girls. I became involved in this network.

Later that year Father Donal O'Mahony, a Capuchin priest who later set up Threshold Housing Agency, asked me if I would visit families in Benburb Street with him and another world opened up. I first visited Benburb Street in 1968 and was to get to know the area, its people and its history very well. The flats were considered luxurious when built by Dublin City Council in 1888. However they had declined over the years and by the 1950s they were designated substandard housing. The rooms were small and suffered badly from condensation. One toilet and one cold water trough served eight families on each floor. Stairs and hallways were dark, and a one-way traffic system brought high density traffic speeding through the street. Local authority tenants evicted else-where were moved to Benburb Street, which became a dumping ground for problem families. Alcoholism, viol-ence, unemployment, petty crime and truancy were

common. The area began to be included on the prostitutes' beat. Older tenants were harassed and fearful.
Vacant apartments were quickly occupied by squatters.

First impressions were mixed. I noticed how comfortable everyone was with Donal O'Mahony and met again
some of the mothers I had nursed in the Rotunda. I saw
that many of the people helped each other as best they
could. I also saw the squalor, the poverty, the needs, and
began visiting regularly getting to know the people. I
remember one night visiting an old lady who hobbled to
the door wrapped in a blanket and leaning on a stick. She
settled down, puffing on a clay pipe with a bottle of
Guinness beside the bed for the night, and we sat over
the burning coals and chatted. I usually left with a
scribbled list of needs and jobs to be done.

Through my involvement in Benburb Street I met girls
who made their living from prostitution. I grew friendly
with one girl who had long black hair. She was from my
native Tipperary. One night she came to my flat, badly
injured, as she had been dragged by her pimp along the
road by her hair. She ended up in hospital and had to have
her hair cut off because of her injuries. Some time later,
meeting her on O'Connell Street, I brought up the subject
of contraception. 'Don't worry, Alice,' she said. 'I'm on the
pill, and I take them all at once so I don't forget!'

During 1969 my basic monthly pay was £67/18s/4d
(£67.91), with £3/10s. (£3.50) extra for night duty. I had
become unsettled at the Rotunda. I was concerned about
how shortstaffed we were, about overcrowding and poor
conditions in the public ward, which was quite unsuitable
for labour management. I was becoming part of a conveyer-

belt system. A mother came; you wrote up her chart; she left. A new mother took her place; you wrote; she left and there was little real contact. I was no longer getting the job satisfaction I needed. I have always felt that contact with patients is the most important thing. I discussed my feelings with the master and matron and was again frustrated at the lack of consultative role for nurses.

Though my work with the adoption society I was becoming godmother to a number of babies and learning of the loneliness, sadness and rejection experienced by many unmarried mothers, some of whom were reared in orphanages or in care. Many homeless people I meet today were reared in orphanages or have children in care themselves.

Change was coming on all fronts. In 1970, nurses marched from Parnell Square to Leinster House to petition the government for better pay, conditions and promotion prospects. At the same time I decided to leave the Rotunda and returned as night sister to Baggot Street Hospital. Some facilities there had improved. The food was better for patients and staff, and the employment of a night cook allowed night nurses to spend more time with the patients. On one tour of night duty I contracted scabies – skin lice. In my work today I meet many people who have scabies and are very ashamed about it. I am able to say, 'Don't worry: I've had it too.'

In 1971 I joined Voluntary Service International, an organisation founded in Switzerland to bring together people of different races and backgrounds to work in social reconstruction projects. The Irish branch of VSI was formed in 1965 and Benburb Street was later adopted as

a social project. Members began wallpapering and painting the Benburb Street flats of old people.

In 1972 VSI conducted a survey of the population in
Benburb Street. There were 519 people living in 139 flats
with as many as five people living in one room. Physical
conditions were deplorable, educational standards low,
unemployment high. The survey caused questions to be
asked in Dáil Éireann. A public official admitted, 'I
wouldn't have a dog living there.' VSI also asked more
philosophical questions, and I quote from the survey:

> Can we not avoid creating another Benburb Street?
> The public experience of substandard housing and
> of eviction to such accommodation of rent de-
> faulters should show that the cost to the taxpayer
> in social welfare, medical services, law enforcement
> and prison maintenance is substantially greater
> than the lost income in rents.

Have we learnt that lesson? The Benburb Street flats are
now long gone but subsequent housing programmes
would indicate that we are still building houses without
community facilities and still herding potentially problem
families together in one place.

Back in the hospital the medical board asked me to
look at intensive care units in London with a view to
opening an ICU in Baggot Street. I spent time in the
London Hospital and also visited hospitals in Sheffield.
In London I joined a student group that came together
to study issues related to the practice of medicine. One
night Cicely Saunders, already well known as the medical

director of St Christopher's Hospice, talked about terminal care. Is it, we debated, about dealing with machines, monitors, ventilators – or is it about people – and how can we get the balance right? This was the first time I had experienced different professions voicing concern for the patient from their particular perspective. It was – and is – a useful approach.

The philosophy I adopted towards intensive care units was promoted by Dr El Borell who worked in a hospital in Georgia and South Carolina. In *The Intensive Care Nurse* he says: 'The key to successful operation of the unit, regardless of the quality of the medical staff, is the kind, intelligent, well-informed and observant nurse.' I returned to Ireland, submitted my report and subsequently set up the intensive care unit. One of the most advanced in the country, it was opened by the Minister for Health, Erskine Childers, and I was appointed sister-in-charge.

In 1972 I took swimming lessons and began a night course in the Russian language and in social science concepts. At the weekend I took children from Benburb Street to the mountains and the countryside. Many had never been in the country before. They fell into rivers, lakes, down hillsides and had a great time. About this time I met Sean Armstrong, field officer for VSI for Northern Ireland. We had met at a VSI party, where a group sat around on the floor and talked. He exuded warmth, care, gentleness. He was one of those special people you meet once or twice in a lifetime. He made a profound impression on me and though he never knew it he was later to alter the course of my life.

During my years in the intensive care unit, various

aspects of the work began to concern me. One was the role of drug companies in medicine. As sister-in-charge, I was regularly invited to receptions organised by drug companies. I began to have reservations about multi-national drug companies' spending of vast sums of money on entertaining the medical profession. It still happens and I wonder if we can truly have an objective and independent health service if practitioners accept such largesse from drug companies?

In hospital the pace seemed to be ever-quicker. Despite an already pressured workload, every six months the ICU received an intake of new junior medical – and nursing – staff who had to be trained in. The constant chopping and changing, never having enough time to reflect on what was happening, too few staff, too many medical represent-atives calling, new admissions – all this created a chaotic work atmosphere.

In 1972 I took leave of absence from the hospital and visited a friend in New Zealand. Before departure I registered as a nurse in England because I felt this could be useful at some future time. I also applied for a full-time social work course at third level and was called for interview to Trinity College. I can still see the woman who assessed me. 'Well, Alice,' she said, 'you have worked so long in hospital, in a very structured discipline; would you really be able to cope with and enjoy life as a student?' I read into this that I was too old to be a student and so she put me off. Or I allowed myself to be put off.

I returned to Baggot Street after three months in New Zealand and did a short course in Transcendental Medit-ation as a means of relaxation. I still use it today. Then on 30 June 1973 my life changed. I got a phone call to say that Sean Armstrong had been gunned down in Belfast a week after his wedding day. I remember feeling absolutely numbed. I spent most of the day crying, walking round the city, thinking about the cruelty of life and the senseless misery caused by evil. Sean Armstrong's death helped me to make up my mind to start working with people in a new way.

The next day I visited the old reformatory at Glencree, County Wicklow, and worked with a VSI group that was restoring and converting the buildings into a centre for reconciliation. I decided I was leaving hospital work and would do voluntary work for some time at least. Two days later a group of us travelled to Belfast to Sean Armstrong's funeral. The church was packed with people of all ages and backgrounds. The one thing we had in common was that we were all crying – mourning the waste and sadness of the loss of this life.

Sean's wife read from Kahlil Gibran's *The Prophet* and there were other inspiring readings. She read a letter from a friend who had a vision the day after Sean's death of a great tree falling, and of little trees growing from it. It is a vision which was to be realised, as his death has been pivotal for many people.

At about this time, I was asked by the Medical Board of Baggot Street Hospital if I would consider accepting the post of matron. I didn't need to consider at all, because I had made up my mind to change direction. I had too many reservations about the structure of hospital nursing, the quality of service to the receiver and the quality of life of the giver. I declined the offer.

So what did I want to do? I thought of the Simon Community, which I knew from my work in Benburb Street. I applied for full-time work with Simon, was called for interview in July 1973 and was accepted. I gave in my notice in Baggot Street and met a variety of reactions. One senior physician suggested I see a psychiatrist. He was not joking. In his eyes, leaving a permanent, pensionable, high-status job in order to go and work for £5 a week with a marginalised community had to mean I was mad.

While waiting to start work in Simon, I did private work in James Connolly Memorial Hospital, Blanchardstown. One day I took a patient by ambulance to the Mater Hospital. We sat in the queue and waited and talked. He described himself as a master chimney-sweep and obviously had a great pride in his work. I realised that this was the first time in a long time I had talked properly to a patient. In September 1973 I joined the staff of Simon. It was the start of a period that was to change my life forever.

7

A STINT WITH SIMON – ALICE

It is after midnight now. The braces are put on the door for the night. The night worker will be up until dawn to let in the stragglers. Those more fortunate are in bed. Others stretch out under the table, on the landing in the hall. Chairs are pulled towards the fire for the telling of tales that will go on until sunrise. We drift into the residential house and sink tired and dazed into chairs around the upstairs fire for the nightly ritual of coffee and cigarettes. We exchange shattered hopes, moments of human kindness and that have made this day whole. As a Simon worker you don't look for success rate or measure progress in terms of months. Many of these people are at the end of the road. You're working in the problem end with many terminal cases and it is soul destroying. But vital.

Irish Press *journalist Tom McPhail, who spent six months as a full-time worker in Simon in 1973 during my time there*

Change is sometimes more difficult for those around us than for ourselves, and this is what I experienced when I decided to work in Simon. I was grateful to my parents for not discouraging me, although they were concerned. It was conveyed to me from some quarters that if you work with 'these people', you become like 'these people'. This is something I continue to hear.

Simon was founded by Anton Wallich-Clifford, who had an infectious ability to see good in all people. Born into a middle-class English Catholic family, he joined the Capuchin Order for a short while and served in the Second World War in the Royal Air Force. He was a voluntary youth worker and journalist, then worked in the British Probation Service. In 1959 he was appointed to the Chief Metropolitan Magistrates Court in Bow Street, London, where he first met homeless people. These men and women affected him deeply.

Anton founded Simon in London in 1963. The organisation takes its name from Simon of Cyrene, who helped Christ carry his cross, and while Christian-inspired, it is ecumenical in action. In February 1969 he spoke to a student group in Dublin, which resulted in a Dublin soup-run one night a week for one hundred people sleeping rough at that time. Later that year the first soup-kitchen was set up in a room in Winetavern Street given by the Franciscan Order. In 1971 Dublin Corporation and the Society of St Vincent de Paul cooperated to make available to Simon a house in Sarsfield Quay at a nominal rent.

Anton Wallich-Clifford died in 1978. I had got to know him well and he stayed with me during one of his visits to Dublin not long before he died. He talked about the

Simon family. One of the things he said was, 'We shall not have changed Skid Row until we have changed society.' It was a privilege to know him.

When I set off for my first day at work in the Simon night shelter in Sarsfield Quay, I had very little luggage. I was met at the door by an old man who kissed me and shook my hand. This was to be a pattern. From the outside, the shelter was dirty and slum-like. Inside it was different. Many residents were very caring towards each other. On my first night a man came up to me and said, 'Why did you mend a hole in my heart which meant I was to end up like this with more problems?' I realised I had nursed him in Baggot Street Hospital.

As full-time workers we shared the same accommodation, food and living conditions as the people we cared for. Our role was wide and varied. It included cleaning, cooking, representing residents in court, visitation of prisons and hospitals, fundraising, administration and being available to listen to and talk to the residents. We were supported by a team of part-time workers.

Simon was run on a tiered system. People who still chose to drink alcohol to excess lived in the night shelter. Adjoining it was the dry house where those who no longer drank heavily lived. A third community moved on to a group home in Harcourt Street. There was a great difference between the dry house and the night shelter. One day I sat with Mary in the dry house. Her room was neat and tidy, with its own chair with a cushion, an ashtray, flowers – in sharp contrast to the crises which often erupted in the night shelter.

There were always cats and dogs in the Simon hostel

and they got a lot of attention. There was a great feeling of belonging. Staff and residents prepared and ate all meals together, as part of the community ethic. There was constant interaction between four groups – the residents, the full-time workers, the part-time workers and the committee – the members of each group being drawn from a wide variety of backgrounds. I was older than the average worker, and for most of the time, the only woman working full-time. I came to see the advantage in being female even in very violent situations. I remember one night a man came in swinging a carving knife. Everyone was screaming and we were very frightened, but I deliberately took a motherly approach to talk him into handing me the knife.

The male staff-worker had a more difficult role. He was seen as the physically strong person in the shelter. His job was to open the door, decide who would come in or stay out, and he inevitably was the one the woman workers turned to for support. Another support for full-time workers was the sensitivity group which met one night a week, set up by psychologist Ian Hart, a long time associate of Simon. He was a member of the government task force on childcare, a man who brought a rare combination of social concern, professional insight and love of people to his work. I remember he visited the shelter one day when I was losing a battle with a blocked sink. I had been shaking DDT over the beds and was about to scrub the floor. As he came in, I had my hands stuck in the sink up to my elbows, shoving a coat hanger down the plug hole to try and clear it. I felt like screaming at him, 'What's the use of social psychology in the middle of all this? What I need now is someone to clear the sink.' It was a question he would have loved!

Ian wrote an article in a Simon newsletter at the time entitled 'Dedicated Volunteer or Mercenary Professional' on the complementary roles of professional and volunteer worker. It remains relevant today:

> Both the dedicated volunteer and the mercenary professional have a place in the Simon Community. The volunteer is needed for his personal commitment to the underprivileged, the professional for his relevant skills and expertise. Without the poorly paid voluntary worker, there might be a growing institutionalisation, and without the professional there might be a tendency to identify with the client to such an extent that the worker might lose his own value.

Ian died in 1980, aged only 40.

Dorothy Goodchild was a voluntary night worker who came armed with home-made shortbread and Woodbine cigarettes for residents. It was good to be on the morning after her night before because everything was left so clean.

One category of professional – the social worker – had great difficulty coping with the Simon philosophy. The training and ethos of social workers often encourages them to attempt to fix a situation. In Simon, we learnt to accept people as they are, without necessarily trying to change them. Working in Simon seemed chaotic but there was order as well. We kept a diary every day. We kept receipts for all monies spent. We discussed what was happening in people's lives through regular staff meetings.

There were sacrifices. For me these were the lack of privacy, not having a clean, warm bed to climb into, no shower, no lock on the toilet door, often no toilet-rolls. But these were only temporary difficulties. Most homeless people are denied some or all of these things on a permanent basis.

We had two days off a week and it was important to get away – particularly from the smells. The smells in Simon drove us all crazy. It was impossible to clean the building adequately. We were constantly frustrated by burst pipes, blocked toilets, seepage through the office floorboards from the sewer underneath. We spent endless time and energy in the fruitless task of trying to keep the building in manageable physical shape.

On a day-to-day basis there were the routine chores of meal preparation, cooking and cleaning which acted as a safety valve. The place was permanently emotionally charged, so the physical work also offered balance and release.

The Simon residents were unique and varied. Jane was haggard after years of rough life and living. Josie sat huddled by the fire, all the time talking about Hitler. Duncan was bearded, kind. One day he sat me by the fire and said, 'I would love to love you but I won't. You are like to so many other people in my life: you will come and you will go.' That sentence has always stayed with me.

John and Mary lived in the Simon house for many years. Often they would not come home and we would be out looking for them. They were heavy drinkers and their circulation was poor. The likelihood of their falling asleep after a few bottles of wine and dying from exposure was very strong. Sometimes we found them in the Coombe area, sometimes sleeping in a shed off the South Circular Road. I remember searching for them one night through the south city and eventually finding them safe and sound. We never did discover too much about their backgrounds. One of the nice aspects of Simon was that people's privacy was respected. We didn't pry into their lives.

Another experience was visiting Mountjoy Gaol, a place I was to get to know well. The waiting-room is usually packed. In some communities the prisoner, the hard man, is a hero. In others, prison is an impediment, a stigma. Over the years, I have found that prison is a home for many homeless people – a place where they receive a degree of respect, a clean bed, food, work, exercise and, most important, a kind of belonging.

Christy Keogh was one Simon resident I visited often in prison. One of the most charismatic men I ever met, Christy had a difficult childhood and spent time in reform schools. He has great powers of survival and can still be hopeful and have fight in him. He was the subject of many emergency meetings in Simon but we learnt a lot from Christy as well. I remember once sitting with him on one of the bridges spanning the Liffey. He was very drunk. To him that day I was three different people. I was his mother whom he blamed for abandoning him; I was all the women whom he wanted to love but was afraid to; and I was myself, a Simon worker.

Simon was in contact with many hospitals. I was in Jervis Street Hospital at 3.30 one morning with a man who had broken a bottle and dashed it into his face. In Doctor

Steeven's Hospital I spent many hours with homeless people who were presenting with cuts and bruises.

There were also visits to courts. I was often in the district court in the Bridewell to speak on behalf of Simon residents who were charged with being drunk and disorderly or for loitering. The court is like a theatre, except that it tends to play tragedy rather than comedy. All – prisoner, gardai, barristers, solicitors, judge – have their role; they have all been through it many times before. Sometimes as I sit in the public gallery, I feel there is a terrible inevitability about the chain of events unfolding below. There is something incestuous about it, each living off the other, each a necessary link in the chain. And the prisoner in the dock is both puppet and puppeteer: he has caused the production; yet he is the most powerless player.

I worked in Simon for six months. I noted when I was leaving that I was glad. I felt that it had been an absolutely marvellous experience for many reasons. Firstly, I had lived on so little for so long. I had given up almost all my privacy as well as time to read, listen to music and meet friends. It was an intense period. If I had not had the experience I would always have been on the outside looking in. But for a while I was on the inside. It was unsafe, challenging, but ultimately very worthwhile. It did not last long but it was an important time in my life and the organisation Trust evolved from it. I wouldn't be doing the work I am today had I not spent six months in Simon twenty years ago.

As I left, I got a taxi and Duncan gave me a pound. He stood on the bridge across the quays crying. He cried and cried, and I cried too.

8

ESTABLISHING TRUST - ALICE

*Trust was born into a society which defined homeless
people in almost exclusively negative and destructive
terms; homeless people by and large described themselves
in similar ways.*

*I had three particular questions which were central to
the ethos of our service. Firstly: could we position ourselves
independently to serve homeless people and yet be con-
nected enough with the relevant voluntary and statutory
services to succeed? Secondly: could we act as a useful
bridge between the person who was homeless and the
various agencies? Thirdly: how would we exercise our
potential role as a voice on behalf of our clients?*

*The ethos which emerged was one in which we acted
as co-experts with our clients. This was profoundly challenging for staff and clients, and is a very different
approach from that generally taken in the fields of
medicine, nursing and social work.*

*Today the position of homeless people in society is
essentially the same as it was twenty years ago. If anything
their alienation is intensified as the economic fabric of*

society slowly breaks down. This catapults greater numbe,
of people on to the borderline and into the abyss of
homelessness.

Trust continues to provide a rich and warm service. The
foundations continue to be alive and relevant. The staff
continue to make themselves present to people who are
homeless, to be witness to their existence, their stories.

David Magee, doctor, psychiatrist, psychotherapist, co-
founder of Trust

When I left Simon I needed two things, a holiday with
space and time to reflect and money to live on in the
short-term. On holiday with a friend in England, I thought
about how nursing and medical facilities could be improved in Simon and realised I was still emotionally
attached to the organisation.

Back in Dublin the post of assistant national director
of Simon came up. I applied and was interviewed. Meanwhile, I worked in a Simon house in Harcourt Street. I
shared a room with a resident, yet another Mary, who was
a colourful and well-known character in the city. Mary
came from a nursing background and was a gentle know-
ledgeable woman despite sometimes bizarre behaviour.
Once, over coffee with me in a city restaurant (dressed
in nightdress and wellingtons), she got up and danced on
the table.

My chores included buying fruit and vegetables from
Smithfield Market, where many traders also donated
produce. We travelled with an old cart which routinely broke
down, scattering cabbages and carrots into the road.

One morning I heard I had got the job of assistant national director and in 1974 I started work in the office of National Simon, working with national director Dick Shannon. I decided to undertake a countrywide survey of the medical problems of homeless people in contact with Simon. This involved an eight-month visitation programme to the Simon shelter, residential house and soup-run, and a wider survey of relevant health boards services. I also sought information from hospitals, GPs, social workers, hostels and other local services.

I began my survey that year. I also visited Simon one night a week with Dr Philip Kennedy, whom I first met in Baggot Street Hospital. Visiting Simon as part of a medical team was both satisfying and frustrating. Living conditions in Sarsfield Quay had worsened. Sometimes there was no running water, the lights fused frequently, it was usually noisy and we often had no facilities in which to examine a patient in privacy.

On average we saw twenty-four people a night. Their medical ailments related to their poor living conditions and years of neglect. These included cuts, bruises, broken bones, leg ulcers, scabies, lice, skin conditions. People needed dressings, stitches inserted and removed. Some had athlete's foot or ingrown toenails; others had minor discomforts such as indigestion. Some were found to need glasses and dentures, and we discovered many serious medical conditions which were not being picked up.

Some of the people we saw were also attending the casualty departments of the city hospitals but often they left before they were properly treated or with a prescription but without the social skills to have it filled, with nobody following up to see how they were.

We spent a lot of time consulting with the staff of hospitals to try to find out what was happening with regard to people who came to us. Many were victims of violence. We often worked in an atmosphere of tension and what we were able to do showed us how much more needed to be done.

One case we encountered was Jimmy, a man in his sixties who had been found by the soup-run sleeping in a telephone kiosk. He was in a terrible state. He was malnourished and absolutely filthy, with swollen ankles and chronic bronchitis. We found he had been discharged from hospital to a city hostel but had been barred for soiling the bedclothes. That night we made a bed for him on a mattress on the Simon office floor, because this was the only space available. We left him a prescription, tended his feet and returned the next day to find him much improved. Subsequently we arranged an appointment with a geriatrician and organised someone to accompany him. He was later accommodated in the Eastern Health Board hospital *Brú Chaoimhín*, in Cork Street. He lived the rest of his days there and died with dignity.

I also think of Larry. One night during my survey I found him sleeping rough, very ill. He had been drinking by the banks of the canal and while he was sleeping a rat had bitten him, and he neglected the bite. After much persuasion and cleaning up, we got him to avail of treatment.

Another night we met a man who had a dog-bite on his left leg. After a few drinks he went to hit the dog but hit his own right leg by mistake. So he ended up with two legs needing attention! Another man had a broken limb which had been set in plaster of Paris for a number of weeks. He couldn't move around and became frustrated. One night he went out the back of the shelter with a saw and cut off the plaster. We found him that night lying in pain and misery and we had to get him quickly to hospital casualty.

One night, all the time and attention in the shelter was given to Skippy, who was having pups. Unfortunately, we had a visiting doctor that night who was very concerned about homeless people. He was not pleased to find the focus of our work was a dog. For me, this was part of meeting people where they were and working with what they considered important.

Over the months we became well-known to homeless people. Near the end of the survey, we were joined by David Magee, another doctor who had worked as a Simon volunteer while a student. A heartening aspect of the work was the number of young highly skilled medical people who offered their services voluntarily. We called the survey report *Medical Care of the Vagrant in Ireland in 1974*. After a lot of consideration we accepted the word vagrant, which the dictionary defines as 'wandering and roving, person without settled home or regular work'.

The main finding of our report was that the breakdown in perceptions between the vagrant and the services can mean that the vagrant is unable to obtain appropriate medical care. The result is a wide range of untreated medical problems among an already socially deprived group.

During the project we built up accurate medical

records on vagrants and by establishing personal relationships with them had made them aware of the medical services and benefits available. We had also made good contacts with medical staff throughout the city. We felt this method of working was an effective model which could be extended nationwide. An added benefit, we felt, would be the easing of problems for hospital medical staff. We recommended the setting up a central body in each health-board region to coordinate the work of the health board, hospital, hostel and community services in providing better medical care for homeless people.

Our long-term recommendations were that more contact between the medical services and homeless people through hostel visitation would be a preventive strategy. We felt that homeless people should be encouraged to apply for medical cards, and that there should be a network of small night shelters relative to local homeless populations.

I submitted my report to the Eastern Health Board. I hoped my findings and recommendations would lead to some action. I hadn't anticipated then how long-term my own involvement would become.

My findings received good coverage on press, radio and television, and, more important, the then Eastern Health Board Programme Manager, Fred Donohoe, responded by agreeing to examine the role of GPs, social medicine departments, medical students and interns in providing a service for homeless people. We also discussed the possibility of appointing someone full-time to coordinate services among homeless people. I said that I would be interested in such a post.

And so it came to pass. I started work for the Eastern Health Board in March 1975 at a net salary of £37.77 per week. The precise conditions of my employment were complex, to say the least. In trying to find a niche for me, Fred Donohoe appointed me temporary staff nurse attached to *Brú Chaoimhín*. I was technically on loan from that section to work in the welfare service of the Eastern Health Board.

In fact, I had nothing to do with *Brú Chaoimhín* and didn't set foot there for years. On one of the few occasions I was there, the gardai were called to order me off the premises, which they declined to do. It happened one night that I was looking for a bed for a woman in their emergency unit. They wouldn't take her in because she was drunk; I said I would not move until they looked after her. They called the gardai to have me ejected.

I am sure there was a considerable perception gap between the way my employers saw my appointment and the way I viewed it. I believe they had visions of my sorting out all the health problems of homeless people, visiting hostels, being motherly, caring, gentle and quiet. I also wanted to use my nursing experience to provide a better quality of life and care for them. I didn't, however, see care only in terms of improved accommodation. I also saw it as a way of being with people. And I certainly wasn't going to be quiet! I took upon myself a freedom to speak out and to highlight issues of injustice. As far as I am concerned, my employers are the homeless population, which means that I see part of my role as taking a stand on their behalf.

My job meant working with three distinct groups –

health-board staff, hostel staff and homeless people. The lives of health-board staffs are very removed from the other two groups. Hostel staffs need support. And homeless people have so many needs. My survey had shown me that the gap between these groups made it difficult for homeless people to have their point of view heard. I saw my role as the link in this chain.

I began work in the health-board offices, then in James's Street, and tried to come to grips with official-dom. People were termed homeless if they lived in a hostels, slept rough or had no fixed abode. Some were labelled homeless even though they had lived in a hostel for many years and regarded it as their home.

At that time there were nine main hostels in Dublin. The oldest is the Model Lodging House in Benburb Street run by Dublin Corporation. The Morning Star Hostel, Morning Star Avenue, and the *Regina Coeli*, for women and children, are run by the Legion of Mary. Then there was the Simon night shelter in Sarsfield Quay, which I knew only too well.

Moving southwards across the Liffey, *Brú Chaoimhín*, Cork Street, had a night shelter for women and children. The Society of St Vincent de Paul run a hostel and temporary night shelter in Back Lane in the Liberties. The Iveagh Hostel in Bride Road offered accommodation for single working men. York House in York Street is a men's hostel run by the Salvation Army.

There were a number of other hostels in the city, many set up to provide accommodation for young country people coming to Dublin to work or to study. Shelter Referral, Merrion Road, was a small hostel for short-term stay. The Dublin Night Shelter for Men in Tara Street closed its doors in 1986.

I also made contact with food centres. These were mainly run by the Catholic Social Service Conference, now called Crosscare. The CSSC had been set up in 1941 by the Most Rev Dr John Charles McQuaid, Archbishop of Dublin, to provide good nourishing food to poor people in the city. Some food centres were already in existence, offering a midday meal at a cost of one old penny. The CSSC refurbished these and expanded the service. Initially I visited all the city's food centres but gradually I began to concentrate on those frequented by homeless people who tended to avoid the busier centres because they didn't like crowds. Many continued to call to presbyteries and convents where they could have a meal in peace and quiet.

My base was changed to Emmet House, Thomas Street, where I had the use of a table and chair. From the beginning, I made it clear that I would respond to the rhythm of the homeless person's day, rather than expecting them to conform to mine. So most of my work was outside the office, meeting people where they were.

I continued to have the voluntary support of doctors Philip Kennedy and David Magee, and Dr Kieran Daly of St Vincent's Hospital joined us, also voluntarily. We were workaholics. Beginning in the early morning we visited hostels on bicycles or on foot and wrote and compiled data. We worked well together; we had great stamina, arguments, debates and discussions. We provided basic first-aid to homeless people and referred some to doctors. We continued to establish contact with GPs and with casualty and social work departments in hospitals.

Key aspects of our work included informing people of their rights and entitlements to, for example, a medical card, social welfare allowances, employment and accommodation. I also aimed to provide people with a range of other services – those of optician, dentist, chiropodist – and with advice on hygiene.

There now enters my story someone who was significant for our future. For years, Ann Rush had worked one night a week on the Simon soup-run. She was well known to many homeless people like Joan, who spent hours walking the streets at night carrying her belongings in dozens of plastic bags. Joan did her washing in three Dublin hospitals, the Richmond, Jervis Street and Baggot Street. It was commonplace to go into the toilets in outpatients and see Joan's long-legged knickers hanging up on a makeshift line. A country woman, Joan had a love for animals and greenery, and Ann would regularly take her to see the deer in the Phoenix Park. Joan later had a room behind the courthouse in Green Street, in the old debtors' prison. Now in her eighties, she lives in a community house.

In 1973 Ann Rush discovered she had cancer and hadn't long to live. She decided she wanted to support our work. A group representing the Eastern Health Board, Simon, the Society of St Vincent de Paul and ourselves began to meet regularly with Ann and her husband Brian and their friend, the solicitor Owen Mulholland, to discuss the possibility of extablishing an expanded service which she might fund.

Finally we agreed to expand our service by employing

a doctor full-time, an appointment which was funded by a private charitable trust set up by Ann Rush. What to call the service? Many suggestions were made before Ann herself came up with the name Trust, and from the beginning, it just seemed perfect. I think unless we trust one another, unless we trust ourselves, we cannot help one another; we cannot live in a peaceful hopeful society if we don't trust. I still see Ann sitting round the polished table in the Vincent de Paul offices as she suggested the name. Even today, I tend to see Trust not just as an organisation or a structure, but as a philosophy of life.

Trust was set up on 25 November 1975 and Ann Rush died in March 1976. Dave Magee and I took turns staying with her at night-time along with her family, and I was privileged to be present when she died.

Trust began in an old health clinic in Lord Edward Street. Dave Magee was employed as a doctor to work with me. We saw our role as providing a small-scale medical social service that in no way duplicated other services. As well as continuing to build up relevant health-board contacts, we also got to know Doctor Brendan O'Donnell, Dublin's MOH, who retired in 1995, a man we feel we can always approach.

We continued to retain an autonomy. Much of the illness we encountered resulted from poor motivation in the people themselves and lack of facilities in hostels. For instance, there was little point in dressing someone's leg ulcer if he didn't have some place to wash his feet. Facilities in hostels were very poor. Bathrooms were open only at certain times; often there were no towels or soap and there was usually no stopper in the bath. Significantly, while time has moved on and technology now rules, the importance of providing the small necessities which make a big difference in people's lives is often overlooked. Today it seems to be easier for an organisation to find the resources for a computer than a bath stopper.

Offering people medical care meant looking to their diet, clothing, footwear and hygiene. Many homeless people washed in toilet blocks in shopping centres and in public toilets. Eventually a bath was installed in our premises in Lord Edward Street. As our work continued, John Long, a social worker, was released from Simon to work with us part-time, and later we had the once-weekly services of a health board psychiatrist. Professor James McCormick, then head of the Department of Community Health at Trinity College Dublin and a member of the Eastern Health Board, became a trustee, and has remained a valuable member of our board since.

In March 1976 Trust produced a document entitled *Report on Broad Medical Service for Single Homeless People in the City of Dublin*, which described in detail how we work, the people we work with, the places we visit and the needs we encounter. Later as part of a response to our report, a day-centre for young people was opened in Henrietta Lane by the CSSC, who were already providing a service for older men. We were involved in its development and management.

The centre initially provided shelter, friendship, recreation and snacks for 18–30-year-olds, mainly homeless. Many of the young people were involved in petty crime and had been in prison or detention centres. Many were poorly educated, and some were illiterate, though only a small number had problems relating to alcohol or drugs.

Our role was to provide a medical and social service for the young people and we had back-up from other agencies.The centre developed very quickly, with a growing emphasis on industrial training programmes. Over the years the role of Henrietta Lane changed; today we are no longer involved but the centre is still going strong.

Our work in Trust brought us in contact with many different bodies. I mention the Department of Justice, the probation and prison service, church groups, Contact, which offered a service to young people, Hope, a young person's hostel, the Samaritans, Alcoholics Anonymous, Gamblers Anonymous, Women's Aid, the Prisoners' Rights Organisation and the Irish Council for Civil Liberties.

In 1979 I obtained a Council of Europe fellowship to study, in the Netherlands, Dutch policy on the rehabilitation of prostitutes, alcohol and drug addicts, and services for migrants.

Of the many interesting encounters on that trip one stands out. It took place in a sex theatre in Amsterdam which I was visiting with members of the Salvation Army who had their headquarters in the red-light district. I was struck by the atmosphere of sadness in an area where people come to find amusement. As I was leaving the theatre, I was grabbed and pulled into a dressing-room. The woman who stood beside me was scantily dressed. She put her hand on my shoulder, burst into tears and spoke in Irish. She said, 'You are Irish, aren't you?' She was from south-east Ireland and she cried and cried as she told me her story. She had obviously been a very attractive woman. She was still young but looked old. Her teeth were decaying, her skin wrinkled, her hair and eyes dull, and she was worn out. Her childhood had been sad. Both parents had been killed in an accident and she had been put in a home. When she left as a teenager she went to London and quickly got caught up in prostitution. She said it was difficult at the beginning but she had no friends, she was a good-looking girl and it was a way of making money. She gradually lost her inhibitions, did well and decided to move to Amsterdam.

At first she made a lot of money but she became dependent on heroin. Her looks faded and business declined. She had now reached the stage where she would love to return to Ireland but felt she could not. She threw her arms around me and said, 'Won't you pray for me?' I am not marvellous at praying but I often think of her. Whenever I go to seminars on poverty, homelessness, prostitution and women's rights, I see her face.

9

A PATTERN OF BEHAVIOUR – PAUL

I was seventeen-and-a-half, angry and confused; I was back in Dublin and I couldn't settle down. I got a job briefly as a waiter in a large hotel but couldn't stick it. I lived with my aunt and uncle who were as kind as possible. I went to see the awful Nana and as soon as I lit up a cigarette she said, 'I knew it: you've given up your religion; you're smoking and you're drinking.' I took pleasure in agreeing that her worst fears had been realised. My heart went out to my young sister Eileen who looked unbelievably lost. All contact with Lillian had been severed.

I couldn't stay in Dublin so I went to work in a hotel in Scotland. I mostly kept to myself and spent time off in my room, reading. I suppressed any unsettling thoughts until one day I was forced to face them. Apparently a young girl in the kitchen had put her eye on me and the hotel porter, a huge, threatening character called Billy, ordered me to date her. We had two very unsatisfactory evenings. Liz was anything but a shrinking violet and must have been disappointed at my lack of response. I lasted in the job about two months. My flight was triggered by a book

I read about homosexuality. Now my feelings had a name, a context, and I was more appalled than before. The answer seemed to be to move on again.

The hotel owners didn't want me to leave. It was high season and I was letting them down. This made me feel even more wretched. I knew I was disappointing people but I couldn't seem to help it. Again I armoured myself with anger against hurt and fear.

I went to London to my brother, whom I hadn't seen since my mother's funeral. He was married and expecting a first child. We went on the town that night and returned very late. That night I told him about my fears of being homosexual and brought up the subject of his years of abusing me. He denied it completely, called me a liar and said if I ever mentioned it again, he would do me an injury. He stormed up to bed and I was left on my own. I knew I was telling the truth but his denial confused me further. I didn't realise then that Daniel was not ready to hear what I had to say.

Soon afterwards, I got a job as a waiter in an hotel in the centre of London. The hotel had a family atmosphere and the owners were very kind. A fellow waiter was George, who became a great friend. One day George asked me if I was homosexual. I was horrified and denied it instantly. George began a relationship with Pamela, a chambermaid in the hotel. He made it clear that he accepted me anyway but I began to feel extremely self-conscious. Did I look different from others? Did I walk in a certain way? Was there something about me? I began to analyse my behaviour and tried to modify my manner. It imprisoned me even more within my head.

George and Pamela were found in bed together and were sacked on the insistence of the manager. I was very lonely without them and wasn't sleeping. A local GP had prescribed sleeping tablets, and one night six weeks after George left I took them all. I had already written and posted a letter to Daniel. It began: 'By the time you get this I will know whether there is a heaven or a hell.' But his wife opened it and got a terrible fright. Meanwhile I had woken up the next morning feeling terrible, and was staggering round the place. I went down to attempt to serve breakfast but it was obvious that I was very ill. I was brought to a hospital and had my stomach pumped.

In the hospital a psychiatrist asked me why I had taken an overdose, and I told him about my thoughts and fears of being homosexual. His response astounded me: 'So what? Be yourself. It's not worth committing suicide over that!' As I listened I saw him through my grandmother's eyes, a pagan Englishman condoning unnatural practices. His attitude confused me more than ever.

Back at the hotel, the owners told me that because of the notoriety my actions had caused, they reluctantly had to let me go. I packed my bags and returned to Ireland, stayed with Jimmy and Joan and came very close to telling Jimmy the reason for my unhappiness. But at the last minute my courage failed me. The taboo around homosexuality at that time was too strong to break.

After a month I returned to England. Dublin was no longer home; the associations there were sad and painful. I had no contact at all with my father, had lost all touch with schoolfriends, and the memories of my mother lingered too strongly. I took a job as a hotel porter in

London. I was miserable, confused and depressed. One night I took an overdose of Aspirin. Again, it didn't work and I was disgusted when I woke up. This time I told nobody, but managed somehow to get through the next day. One of the staff thought I was drunk and asked me if I had been to an Irish wake. I said yes and that I had drunk a lake.

I'm not sure whether my suicide attempts were serious efforts to take my own life or just cries for help. The threat of homosexuality loomed constantly. I felt incapable of doing anything about it. I felt there was nowhere I could go for help. I wanted nothing to do with such a nature yet I seemed to be saddled with it.

Once again I ran away. I came back to Dublin and got a job in a small city hotel. I was working a sixteen-hour day and became exhausted. The owner was most unpleasant. One morning she came into the dining-room where I was resetting tables after breakfast. She said, 'I can feel the grains under the tablecloths. The tables haven't been swept properly. Do it again.' I cracked up. I pulled off all the tablecloths, got a bucket, deck brush and Vim and began to scrub the tables, ruining the surfaces completely. I began to laugh and cry and when the owner came in, I ordered her out of the room. The dam had finally burst and anger poured out.

I don't remember too much more about that day. I went to the doctor and at his suggestion agreed to go to hospital. I was given lots of tablets – anti-depressants, sleeping pills, tranquillisers. At first it was wonderful. There was a tremendous feeling of relief that I had finally let go. I was floating around with no troubles.

One day I was sitting with a woman patient called

Heather, when we saw two staff members hauling off a screaming woman. I said, 'She should be in a loony bin,' and Heather replied, 'Where do you think this is?' I had no idea I was in a psychiatric hospital and I was shocked. Growing up, I had inherited all the attitudes which attach a stigma to mental illness.

I was in hospital for four months. My father visited me once and we had nothing to say to each other. My first experience of Irish psychiatric care was notable for the lack of care it offered. I was a difficult patient, introverted and very suspicious. Yet none of psychiatrists I saw ever asked me why I had a nervous breakdown or what my real problems were. One day I was told I was going home, that I would continue to attend out-patients and receive medication. I was shocked and frightened about leaving hospital. Joan and Jimmy had moved house and did not have room for me. I returned to my grandparents' house because I felt I needed some security.

As soon as he saw me, my grandfather came right to the point: 'I hear you've been in the loony bin,' he said to me as we sat in the kitchen. 'Well, I don't know why you've come back here because this is another madhouse.' My grandmother's greeting was equally typical: 'I didn't come to see you in hospital because none of my family was every mentally sick,' she said. 'You must have got it from your mother's side.'

After a few weeks I took a job in a public house in the city centre and got through the days somehow. The pills were becoming a great crutch and I was living life in a bit of a fog. On Good Friday that year I was walking home late when a man in a car stopped and offered me a lift.

We began to talk and I was amazed and frightened at the powerful feelings he evoked in me. He stopped the car and kissed me. He wanted to go further but I was absolutely terrified, got out of the car and ran away. The next day I was serving drinks as usual in the bar when the door opened and in walked last night's stranger. I almost fainted. I ran up to the restroom and stayed there until he left. Shortly afterwards, I gave in my notice as the place had become too dangerous for me.

Emotionally I was in a very bad state. I felt I had gone a little bit further down the road to homosexuality but then had retreated sharply. I was taking lots of pills and they were helping to blur reality. Soon afterwards I suffered another loss. My grandfather became ill, went into hospital and died unexpectedly. I took the call from the hospital. When I told my grandmother and asked if I would make a cup of tea for us both, her answer was chilling. She said, 'No, he's gone now; that's the end of it,' went back to her room and closed the door. I stayed up all night crying. I loved my grandfather and he made all the difference to living in that house.

One day, soon after his death, I went to the suitcase where my father kept his savings and stole £50. I spent it going to the pictures day after day. There was a great fuss made about the theft and a few weeks later I did it again. My father accused me of stealing, I admitted it and said he was never getting it back. There was a huge row and I returned to psychiatric hospital. I had been wanting to go there anyway and probably engineered the row so that I could go back. It was safe, a place to run to, and it would become both refuge and prison for many years.

10

THE 1980s – ALICE

If members of society find it difficult to identify with inequalities, others have to do it for them – be it politicians, care workers or journalists. On a personal level, each individual who works in the media has a professional and moral responsibility to ensure that all relevant points of view are included and items which concern the voiceless are not omitted.

In practice those who are voiceless are usually poor and powerless. They have no disposable income and are of less interest to sales and marketing sectors. Neither advertisers in search of consumers nor newspapers in search of readers nor broadcasters in search of audiences are materially motivated to cater for the needs of the voiceless.

In practice the voiceless threaten the security of powerful forces in society and giving them a voice is likely to alarm those who control power and resources. It can also be very disturbing for consumers to hear the human sounds of suffering on their own doorstep. Close-to-home misery is also close to the bone.

Of course those who work in the media cannot escape

sharing to some extent in the same prejudices as those of society in general. They have a job to do and it is often easier to cater to the mainstream. In the end of the day people not only get the government they deserve. They get the media they deserve.

Colm Kenny, Senior Lecturer, Communications Department, Dublin City University, on the responsibility of the media to give a voice to voiceless people

The 1970s had been a decade of growth and expansion. The hope for the 1980s was that this would continue. A prophetic note was struck, however, in April 1980, when Margaret Gaj closed her restaurant. It was situated on a first floor in Baggot Street and for twenty-one years Margaret had presided over a meeting-place which became as much club as café. You would see all kinds of people there – journalists, tourists, travellers, unemployed people, prostitutes, politicians, business people, actors, civil-rights activists. The colourful mix seemed to encompass the spirit of a time when barriers between differing groups were being broken down. When it closed, many of us felt we had lost something special.

In March 1980 the story of a homeless girl called Rachel had a happy ending. Rachel was English, in her late twenties, and had slept out in Dublin for over two years. I heard of her through the gardening staff in St Stephen's Green. Various bodies put pressure on me to have her committed to a psychiatric institution but she told us that fears of psychiatric in-patient treatment was one of the reasons she was sleeping out.

We let her be – with support. I visited every day, as did Captain Mary Miller of the Salvation Army and the Simon soup-run. The gardai were kind to Rachel and worked with us. After some months she moved to a Salvation Army hostel, and was allowed take with her the stick she felt she needed for protection even though it was against regulations. She began attending a psychiatric day centre and applied for and received a supplementary welfare allowance. Gradually her appearance improved: she changed her clothes, washed and cut her hair and finally she got rid of the stick herself when she felt she didn't need it any more.

Rachel eventually made contact with her parents in England. They were overjoyed to hear from her and she flew home. Her story illustrates the value of people working together using a personal approach. It also highlights the important role often played by non-professionals (such as the staffs in public parks) in the wider care of homeless people.

In 1980 a social service agency was established in the Pro-Cathedral, which became an important focal point for homeless people. Now known as Centre Care, it was formerly called Open Door.

By this stage Dave Magee had left Trust to study psychiatry and had been replaced by Dr Laurence McGibbon. Laurence had worked in St Brendan's Hospital, and therefore brought a new expertise to Trust. He was a great listener. His approach was gentle and sensitive and he was totally at one with our philosophy in not labelling anyone mentally ill.

In 1981 we moved to the basement of the Iveagh

Hostel, renting it from the Iveagh Trust at a nominal rent of £1,000 per year which has never been increased. In planning the move we involved the people we work with so as to cause them the minimum of stress. The Iveagh is a beautiful old building, and the location is very suitable for our work.

In 1983 Paddy Gallagher came to work with Trust and Jackie Hayden joined us for a time. Much more than another pair of hands, she was young and caring, and brought a femininity to the work. Janet McDermott, a nursing sister in the Adelaide Hospital, was a tremendous support also at that time. In 1985 Laurence McGibbon left us to work in child psychiatry in Britain. We took time to assess the gap his departure created. Over the years community care services for homeless people had improved. Many had medical cards and we encouraged them to use the GP of their choice. We had also built up a relationship with local doctors, particularly Oliver Connolly and John Latham. We decided not to employ a doctor full-time, a decision which we have held to. Paddy Gallagher joined us full-time in 1986.

During the 1980s several issues brought us into continuing contact with the health board and politicians. The first related to the community welfare service. Most people we worked received their payments and information on housing and social welfare issues from the Eastern Health Board offices in Lord Edward Street. In 1983 the board planned to transfer this service to Benburb Street, two miles away. I was part of a professional group that publicly expressed concern about the move which was taken without consultation with clients or with the many services that work with clients.

On the week of the move, a welfare officer visited the Iveagh Hostel and pinned up a notice announcing the move, written with a blue ball-point pen on a dark-brown piece of cardboard. When criticism was voiced about the inadequacy of this means of notifying people of fundamental changes in a crucial service, the notice was later replaced with a larger piece of cardboard inscribed with a larger handwritten sign. The move involved extra travel for recipients which, combined with payment of allowances by cheque instead of cash, caused much confusion and stress. Eventually the Community Welfare Service for homeless people in Benburb Street closed and moved to its present address – the old TB clinic in Charles Street, a more convenient location for clients.

The issue highlights the gap between service-planners and service-users. I believe many caring people within the statutory services are aware of this gap but feel they cannot speak out because of the terms of their employment. So they stay and may grow a layer of indifference for their own protection, or they leave. My work continues to bring home to me the need to speak out on behalf of many who cannot do so and the importance, therefore, of an independent voice like Trust.

My work at that time covered the entire city area and suburbs. I met up to 300 people a week. I visited all hostels weekly, with regular spot-checks at night-time. There were also visits to bus stations, parks, derelict sites, squats, skippers. The people I was in contact with represented a large number of psychiatric and ex-TB patients, ex-prisoners, drug addicts, alcoholics, pregnant women, and included some very inadequate, dependent people with long-term problems. Some homeless people who are homosexual can encounter discrimination from their own community as well as from society at large.

In Trust we had students on placement from the nursing, medical and religious professions. Most middle-class students had little understanding of the reality of life for homeless people, and some remained rather blinkered in their views. One who came as a student has remained a firm friend. Colm Harte had trained as a social worker before enrolling to study medicine in UCD as a mature student. I remember after one long, difficult day in Trust, he turned back before going out the door and asked: 'Alice, what keeps you going?' And I remember my reply: 'The people themselves.' Colm now works as a Dublin GP and his expertise is always available to us.

Conor was another person who changed during his time with us. He was a clerical student and this is part of his report to us:

In the past, homeless people for me existed only as drunkard, bum, noisy tramp or beggar – all of whom got in my way on a bus, at a film, or having a meal. I had nothing in common with them at all.

I tried to have as little to do with them as I could. Despite this I considered myself to be caring. While I felt Christian, I felt no guilt about the fact that all I did was turn away. I felt it was a problem the state should look after.

I have changed . . . homeless people are now part of my life. I think about them even when I am away from them. I am more understanding and caring and see myself in many of them. I see them as very hurt people just trying to make do.

A major area of concern in the 1980s was drug testing. We had noted the numbers of homeless people attending drug trials, being used effectively as guinea pigs, and consenting to it because they were being paid. We knew the need for drug trials; our concern was with the people used, often poor, poorly educated, with addiction problems. In 1984 I co-founded a Social Policy Action Group which initiated a national debate on drug testing. We produced a pamphlet *Human Drug Trials – A Cause for Action*. In it we highlighted the fact that legislation regarding drug testing did not provide adequate safeguards for volunteers against potential risks and abuses. We told the stories of some of the people we had met. Typical was James, an unemployed former drug addict, who participated in trials in order to get money to buy drugs. He had no difficulty smuggling in drugs and injecting himself with heroin during the drug trials, activities which were either ignored or unnoticed by the screening system.

In 1984 the tragic death of a young man involved in a drug trial highlighted many of the problems we had been publicising. New legislation concerning drug trials was being considered and we made a submission to the Minister for Health regarding its provisions. We felt financial incentives to volunteers or recruiters should cease, and that an independent ethics committee should be appointed to supervise protocol, administration and recruitment. In 1985 new legislation regarding drug trials was passed and many of our recommendations were taken on board.

In spring 1985 Simon's night shelter in Sarsfield Quay was demolished as a dangerous building. That same year Sister Stanislaus Kennedy set up Focus Point to help people to find and maintain a home, if they were out of home or threatened with homelessness. When she first came to Dublin, I took her round the hostels, introduced her to many of my colleagues and gave her a feel for the situation of the homeless at that time. Focus Point has developed into an agency which concentrates much of its effort on young people, and under its umbrella there are sheltered housing complexes, social work services, youth training and personal development opportunities.

The work of Sister Stanislaus was timely in that the 1980s saw the emergence of a new type of homeless person – young, perhaps a runaway from a broken home, from family abuse, sexual abuse, violence or neglect.

In 1984 about twenty voluntary organisation had formed the National Campaign for the Homeless to improve conditions for homeless people. In autumn 1985 they organised a seminar in Cork at which Brian Harvey of Simon gave an overview of Irish homelessness at the time. There were an estimated 3,000 homeless people in the country, with 300 of these sleeping rough in doorways, laneways, cars and sheds. About 2,700 were in hostels and night shelters, some in psychiatric units with discharge out of the question because of homelessness. He continued: 'Legal protection for the homeless person is virtually non-existent. Homeless people are, in fact, criminals under the vagrancy laws, which make it a crime to beg or "wander abroad without visible means of support".' He said many housing authorities refused to house some categories of homeless people and referred them to a health board, who in turn regarded homelessness as a housing matter and sought to refer them back to the housing authorities.

Peter McVerry SJ spoke on 'Public Attitudes to the Homeless'. He said:

A small proportion of those who become homeless have personal problems that will not be solved solely by the provision of accommodation. They have reached the final stage of a process of social decline, a reaction to unemployment, poverty and personal crisis with which they have been unable to cope adequately. But again, we must focus on the fact that their plight is not solely traceable to individual failing but also due to the inability of society's support systems society to deal adequately with such problems at an early stage. The problem of homelessness is essentially one of social injustice.

In the autumn of 1985 I received a letter from Richard, a homeless man on remand in Mountjoy Gaol.

Just a few lines to say I am in prison for breaking into a pub for drink. I never took any money, only spirits. Alice, I have a chronic drink problem and I am powerless to help myself. I tried. I signed myself into St Brendan's, I went to an alcoholic unit in

Cork. But on leaving I had nowhere to go or no one to turn to. Subsequently I was back on the drink. I am a good worker and a skilled tradesman. I need help. Alice, you understand what it's all about. Will you speak for me in court? I would be very thankful.

I duly spoke up for Richard and he got off. We tried to get him work but in a few weeks he was back on the drink and stopped calling to Trust. We got a message to him to say that he would always be welcome. We find people feel they owe us something if we put effort into helping them and they subsequently fall by the wayside. People owe us nothing: their first duty is to themselves. If they can change their lives, let them do it for their own sakes.

In January 1986 there was a staff strike in the Iveagh Hostel. It began as an unofficial action by one of two hostel painters who claimed he had been made redundant while his colleague – soon to retire – was kept on. The strike became official. The hostel's 150 residents had no security of tenure and worried about eviction. We continued to look after their medical needs and hear their many fears. Upstairs, too, staff worried that the hostel would be closed. The Iveagh had fallen into poor repair and massive resources would be needed to upgrade it. Bed, bath, dining and leisure facilities were very poor; however, for many it was home.

RTE picked up the story. A reporter knocked on our door to ask us for a comment. We decided it was important that the residents be heard, and one of them, Tim McDermott, now in his eighties, told his story very simply.

He had then lived in the Iveagh for fifty years. Despite its shortcomings, it was his home; he could see no life outside it for him or for many others. The programme went out on the radio news that day, and an hour later the strike was called off.

The official reason given was that the staff could not abandon the residents. We did not blame the staff. We said at the time that such situations would not arise if there was a proper policy and funding provision for homeless people at government level.

In February 1986 I received a letter from a homeless woman friend, Mary, looking for help. A flat had been found for her and her family but she was destitute and had no money to furnish it. I got in touch with Willie Birmingham, the fireman who had founded Alone to help elderly people. Willie cared fiercely for the people he helped. He felt they needed not charity but justice. With his wife Marie and family and his colleague Liam Ó Cuanaigh, he did much to raise national awareness on many poverty issues. He died in April 1990.

In early September 1986 I spent a week on the island of Iona off the Scottish coast participating in a course organised by an ecumenical body, the Iona Community, entitled 'An Exploration of Some Contemporary Issues in Health Care'. One of the most useful exercises was taking part in role-play as members of a health board – our task to save £2m. I 'resigned' from the board at the end of the session, refusing to accept the cuts until plans for community services were made available.

In September 1986 the old TB clinic in Charles Street was closed. Changing times and better healthcare meant that Dublin ceased to have any walk-in TB clinic and patients would now be referred to a general hospital. However, in Trust we must remain vigilant regarding TB, as its incidence among homeless people tends to be higher than among the general population.

Matt could be a case in point. He had been a heavy drinker for years, lived rough and in hostels. When we were treating him for a serious burn, he told us he had been coughing up blood for months. After much reassurance he agreed to see a doctor who diagnosed TB. He was admitted to hospital for treatment. Before Matt was discharged, arrangements were made for him to return to his family and to continue to be treated locally. However, on leaving hospital he received his accumulated allowances and blew the lot on drink. He never reached home, was found sleeping rough again and landed back in hospital.

There was also a case of the two brothers who had lived in hostels and finally got a flat in Rialto but it had a happier outcome. When we visited them they had nothing except an old stove, on which sat a frying pan with a few burnt rashers. Luke, one of the brothers, had TB, and we finally persuaded him to go to the doctor. We were told his medication needed to be monitored daily, including weekends. So every Friday night Paddy made contact with Luke, opening up Trust for him on Saturday morning, giving him breakfast, seeing that he had a wash and a change of clothes and giving him his medication. This continued for months until Luke was clear.

In Trust we constantly receive requests for information on homelessness. In 1987 we produced a booklet (since reprinted), to explain who we are, how we think and what we do. We offered the philosophy of Trust, which is based on two central principles: the recognition of every individual's right to be treated as an autonomous and unique human being, and the need to restore the dignity of people whom society has labelled deviant and undesirable.

We explained how Trust operated, described the kinds of problems homeless people encounter, the medical aspect of our work, the back-up support services we can call on and, with their permission, told the stories of nine people we meet. We saw our booklet as part of our public education policy. In it, Professor James McCormick, chairman of Trust, describes the nature of homelessness:

Homeless is merely a symptom of a much more deep seated set of problems. For this reason the solution to these problems is more complex and difficult than the provision of housing.

If these problems have a common factor it has to do with a failure to become or to remain a part of the wider community. Homeless people are largely viewed as failures who are to blame for their own misfortunes.

The reality is, of course different. Once set on a downward path, often as a result of things over which they have no control, such people may readily enter a spiral which ensures that they become more and more distanced from their fellow citizens and have less and less in common with those who have loving families, a home and a regular income.

It is not surprising that there are no simple
solutions to such problems. The provision of a flat
does not solve their difficulty. What is needed is
a slow and painful rehabilitation which has as its
main objective restoring a sense of personal
worth. This takes time and patience.

In 1987 the Adelaide Hospital closed its casualty department. One of the tragedies of the 1980s was the closing
of so many voluntary hospitals in Dublin and around the
country. Between 1980 and 1990, Dr Steeven's Hospital,
Jervis Street, the Richmond, Mercer's, Baggot Street, Sir
Patrick Dunn's all closed their doors. Baggot Street has
continued as a community hospital, Mercer's has a GP
practice and Dr Steeven's Hospital is now the headquarters of the Eastern Health Board. These hospitals gave
employment to local communities and offered a caring,
city-based service. In December 1987 Trust highlighted,
among other issues, the unplanned moves of psychiatric
patients from hospitals to hostels which we had begun
to witness as a growing problem.

Autumn 1988 was a significant time in my life. I got
married and I received a People of the Year Award
sponsored by the Rehabilitation Institute. Receiving
awards with me were Jack Charlton, Gordon Wilson,
Carmencita Hederman, Ollie Jennings and Norma Smur-
fit. While I felt honoured and gratified, one of the most
useful outcomes was the facility RTE offered us to
produce a video about our work.

In September 1989 Dublin Simon Community formally
moved into new premises at Usher's Island. The purpose-

built shelter has thirty beds, providing emergency short-term accommodation for men and women. On the same site there is also an eleven-bed long-term residential community house for Simon residents. Usher's Island also became the headquarters for the community's soup-run which, every night of the year, brings soup, tea, sandwiches, blankets, clothing and friendship to up to thirty people sleeping rough.

Looking back on the 1980s, I remember that many times I considered giving up, because of the frustration I experienced in dealing with aspects of the health service and the realisation that Trust was a small voice battling constantly against a hamstrung bureaucracy. While individual officials can be caring, the system tends to be uncaring. But something always happened to keep me going. Someone we hadn't seen for years would wander in and was the better for seeing us. Or I might meet a colleague who shared our vision. Or, in spite of the system, I would recommit myself to homeless people and decide that the battle is worthwhile. I believe that in so far as we have some truth and knowledge, we need to keep on expressing it, need to keep on speaking up for those who can't speak for themselves.

11

THE PSYCHIATRIC MERRY-GO-ROUND – PAUL

After the row with my father I went back to hospital, stayed for four months and came out less well, more dependent on pills and more jittery than when I had gone in. Hospital solved nothing. Nobody was challenged there, no issues addressed. A woman patient fancied me but instead of being flattered I was terrified. However, hospital was still a place to run to, a place to hide.

When I was discharged I found a flat. There was no going back to the family. I had severed connections with them after my grandfather's death. My father had re-married, choosing someone my mother had never cared for. I felt that his marriage was a betrayal of her and it alienated him from me even further. I was lost, aimless, lonely.

Gradually a pattern established itself. I would get a job in a pub or restaurant but after some weeks or months find myself attracted to a male staff member or regular customer. I couldn't cope with it and would run – into hospital. This began to change when I became a patient of Dr Noel Browne. From the beginning he was different.

He began by asking me why I was on so much medication. I said indignantly, 'Because I'm sick,' and thought him stupid. He said I didn't need all the pills and that he was going to reduce them. I said, 'And how the hell am I going to sleep?' And he said, 'I'm going to give you a twenty-four-hour pass and you're going to walk and become physically tired like everyone else.' I thought he was completely crazy, so convinced was I at that time that I was sick and needed constant medication. I remember saying to him, 'You're mad,' and he answered: 'There's a distinct possibility you may be right!' He also said, 'You're not a patient; you're a person,' which scared the life out of me. I felt safer as a patient.

He was, however, successful in gradually weaning me off medication. I felt much better. We discussed my sexuality briefly and he gave me advice about self-acceptance. He also encouraged me to be more open with my family and so I wrote a letter to everyone, explaining my worries about homosexuality. But no member of the family replied, which hurt me a lot. I told myself I didn't need them.

Soon after leaving hospital I had my first full sexual experience with a man. I met someone in a pub and we went back to his place and went to bed together. I liked the closeness of being held and found it very emotional. But my feelings were still hugely ambivalent. It was as if I were acting, observing myself from the sidelines. I was thinking, 'Well, everyone says this is the way I am, so I'll go with it and see what happens.' But there were also feelings of guilt and revulsion. The other man wanted to continue seeing me but I refused. He worked in a bank and gave me a glimpse of the double life he was living, hiding his orientation from the people he worked with, which seemed to be a terrible strain.

The flight continued and soon after that I ended up in hospital again. There something very important happened. I met another patient, Ruth, who was being treated for anorexia. She took my breath away she was so beautiful, and we fell in love.

She left hospital before me but I was able to visit her on a day-pass. I was very interested in her family life, in its openness and relaxed approach. We began a brief sexual relationship and although I was delighted to be in love and felt at last I had something to live for, the other dark feeling wasn't gone; it was just in cold storage, pushed down but not out.

My time with Ruth was short-lived. Although she loved me she didn't want a heavy relationship then and needed to get away from Ireland. Her going away devastated me; I drifted in and out of hospital and some time later I moved to a new unit to undergo a course of aversion therapy. The aim was to 'cure' me of my so-called homosexuality. The treatment sounded pretty unpleasant but I agreed to go along with it because I decided I would put up anything if this awful thing left me.

My aversion therapy involved looking at pictures of naked men and naked women. If I lingered on a picture of the naked men, or men undergoing pain or humiliation, I received an electric shock, although I was allowed to gaze at length at pictures of naked women without receiving shocks. Over the weeks the shocks became increasingly strong. The treatment came to be a horrible, obscene experience. You knew you were going to be hurt and there was the anticipation and degradation of pain, as well as the pain itself. At this stage I was back on all medication again. Noel Browne had left the hospital and I missed him.

The unit was run on very militaristic line. Tokens which entitled patients to food and socialising were earned by 'good' behaviour and withheld for 'bad' behaviour. Rules were rigidly applied. Someone with no tokens could receive only Complan and bread and butter, a regime that could last for days. One man had only Complan on Christmas Day, other food being withheld by over-zealous staff working under a controlling doctor.

I celebrated my twenty-first birthday in the unit but after a few months, the control and manipulation got to me and I knew I had to get out of the place. I felt the aversion therapy was harming me. We were told we would be allowed to leave only if we got a job. I went out one day determined to come back with a job, and proof of a job. This I did. I signed up for the Irish Navy in Cork, not having a clue what I was getting myself into. That night I returned to the hospital flaunting the documentation and they had to let me go. I packed my bags, told them all what I thought of them and left. Someone ran down the road after me with a month's supply of tablets. I fed them to the fish in Cobh.

Naval training in Cobh lasted four months. I was put in the hotel group and managed quite well. I didn't socialise too much but spent a lot of time lying on my bunk reading.

Physically I was getting into shape. I was off medication and the training was doing me good. I refused to go to Mass and for this was put on orderly duty which usually meant cleaning the toilets. Another punishment was to run around the square with a heavy object held over your head. This weighed a ton on your seventh or eighth time round the square, so I began to develop strong arm muscles as well!

A week before my passing-out parade I had some time off and came to Dublin. I called to see Joan and Jimmy and also met a childhood friend, Gerard, who was still living with his very over-protective mother. He grew very excited about my tales of naval life and decided to join up with me. I tried to discourage him but his mind was made up. He went home, packed his bags and we left the next morning with his mother running down the street after us, calling me a so-and-so son-stealer.

By the end of the first day, I knew Gerard wouldn't make it in the navy. He said he couldn't stand people shouting at him all the time. As each day passed he grew worse and I used to find him down by the wharf staring in at the water threatening to jump in or desert and go to England. He wouldn't last a day in England on his own. I felt I had to stand by him. We deserted and left for London. So here I was on the run again, this time motivated by caring for someone else. In some ways I was sorry to be leaving. I was about to be passed out after my initial training, but I felt I had no choice. I had to look after Gerard.

We arrived in London and were no sooner fixed up in two live-in hotel jobs than Gerard wanted home. I organised things for him and sent him on his way. Meanwhile I looked up my friends, George and Pamela, now married with a child. It soon became clear to me that George was carrying on with other women. Pamela knew, too, and it was sad to see a couple that I thought so much of hurting each other. It was the last time I was to see them. When I next tried to make contact I was told they were not known at the address and there was no forwarding address. I never knew what happened to them. I assume the marriage broke up as Pamela was not the type of woman to share her man with anyone else.

I decided to face the music at home. I was escorted to Cobh by armed gardai from Dublin, where I was fined but not expelled. However, I decided to leave of my own free will. I had had enough. I had to stay on to earn my fines and pay back the cost of my uniform which had been stolen. Then I left the navy. Looking back, even though I was in an all-male environment there were no sexual issues for me, which is probably just as well. Two men had been caught together during my time there. They had been expelled, publicly humiliated and their families and parish priests had been contacted.

Back in Dublin another homosexual encounter preyed on my mind and landed me back in psychiatric hospital. I escaped on the second night, pretended I was taking a bath but left through the window, throwing my clothes out in front of me and jumping out naked into a freezing winter evening. I went to a priest friend who had helped me from time to time. He put me up in a bed-and-breakfast place for a week and tried to talk to me. But I suppose he wasn't getting through to me. After a week I told him I had found somewhere and asked for a loan of £50 for a deposit. I spent the money on barbiturates, took an overdose and went into a coma. It was another cry for help. I was brought to St James's hospital, had my stomach pumped and felt wretched for some days. In St James's, however, I met another good doctor, young, caring, go-ahead. As with Noel Browne, he took me seriously, and after some weeks of working with me, gave it as his opinion that there was nothing psychiatrically wrong with me. He persuaded me to organise and facilit- ate a daily discussion group. Participants were given a certain amount of independence. We made our own beds and we were allowed passes out to go to films.

The doctor also offered me a desensitising programme to help me know my fears and face them. Under the influence of a tranquillising drug, he introduced me gently and slowly to simulated situations which I found difficult and encouraged me to feel the fears and work through them out the other side. This was very helpful, and we were making progress until it was realised that I was becoming addicted to the drug, and so the treatments had to be discontinued in that form.

I spent Christmas 1974 in St James's Hospital but eventually it was time to leave with no follow-up activity other than the facility of attending out-patients once a week. So one day you were in hospital, safe, secure, warm, fed, all decisions made for you. The next you were on the streets, cold, frightened alone, very unsure of being able to cope on your own. Predictably I went downhill fast. This time I bought some blades, went back to the base- ment of my old home and slit my wrists. I remember rubbing my arms against the door and seeing the blood run down. The next morning very early I went to the

Samaritans and they got me into St Patrick's Hospital. My stepmother came in to see me. I was very woozy and when I woke up I saw she had left Agatha Christie's *By the Pricking of My Thumbs*, a fairly ironic choice, though this was probably lost on her.

In St Patrick's I had ECT (electro-convulsive therapy). You are given an anaesthetic and when you come round, it is as if nothing has happened. But you feel so out of it you hardly know your own name. Gradually things come back but gaps remain. As it was explained to me then, the aim of ECT was to blot out whatever has been troubling you as if it never had been. It worked. It wiped out much of my past, I forgot it for years. It was also socially inconvenient. People would greet me in the street and I hadn't a clue who they were.

The effect was disquieting. I felt incomplete, split off from myself, alien. It was also very stressful. I had to hide my memory gaps. And as part of my problem those days was hiding my true thoughts and feelings, another layer of pretence was now added.

One day I was listening to two patients talking and it was all 'my doctor', 'my treatment'. I realised 'My God, I know nothing else but doctors! Is this all there is? If so, I'm not going to have it any more.' I took a whole bottle of the pills. This time I meant it. I woke up with pain in every part of my body and a trip hammer knocking in my brain. I was brought by ambulance to Jervis Street, transferred back to a psychiatric hospital and signed myself out after a few days.

I left hospital determined not to return. I got a job as a waiter in an hotel outside Dublin and stayed there for over a year, the longest time I had ever held down a job. I had also stayed out of hospital for thirteen months, managing all this by leading a controlled and very regimented life. I was twenty-five years old. Now a new chapter was about to open.

12

A JOURNEY IN TRUST (1)

A lot of homeless people are victims of changes in society. Some had good jobs but due to the break-up of relationships, loss of job or addiction they were unable to cope, became ashamed and were eventually ostracised. A cruel society demands success as a passport to acceptance.

As we moved into the late '70s and early '80s, the rigid structures which had bounded the nation together were loosened. Attitudes to church, marriage and human dignity changed. Crime increased. The family came under increased pressure. Drugs added mayhem to cities. These changes spawned more homelessness.

How can we improve the service? First, we need to acknowledge that a problem exists. We need public education so that homeless people are not branded as useless, dossers or criminals. We need to create an awareness that these are people who have fallen on hard times and are suffering partly because of the distrust of society. The move towards integration between health, social welfare and housing departments is timely. With today's technology it should be possible to identify homeless people and

*introduce a coherent plan of action to improve the quality
of their lives. What we still need, however, is the political
will.*

Garda Inspector Tim Doyle

It is eight o'clock on a Wednesday morning. In the Model
Lodging House in Benburb Street, the large bare dining-
room is fairly empty. A few men sit round smoking and
drinking tea. Some are chatting together in groups; others
sit alone staring into space. Martin is at the hatch inside
the front door, and receives the £1 from people booking
their night's accommodation in advance. The hostel has
eighty-four beds. Some residents are long-stay and now
pay by the week. Inside the office, the superintendent,
John Hayes, greets the residents. The building is dark,
cheerless, very poorly furnished and in need of redecor-
ation and refurbishment – which is in the pipeline.
Dublin's oldest hostel opened its doors in 1888 and the
building has changed little in that time. But the atmosphere is pleasant. The staff say goodbye to people they
know. There is some feeling of belonging.

As I stand in the hall a young man comes in the front
door with a large rucksack on his back and, eyes down,
mounts the stairs quickly to the dormitory above. He is
the son of a wealthy Dublin family, and he has been
sleeping rough for some time. An older man wants to talk.
He suffers from epilepsy and would like his own flat. His
pockets are bulging with bottles of tablets. He says he has
to take them everywhere with him, as they would be stolen
in the hostel. I invite him to Trust for a proper chat.

In the dormitories the lack of privacy is apparent. Each resident has a bed in a wooden cubicle. That's all. No storage, no lockers, no wardrobes. Residents hang their clothes up as best they can on the walls of their cubicles. Black plastic bags bulge out from under some beds, holding more possessions. Down the stairs are the toilets, bathrooms and showers. There are no towels or soap as people are expected to provide these themselves, though they will be supplied by the superintendent if requested. The reason given for not having them available is that they would be stolen.

A man appears at the hatch, anxious and excited. He lives in a Corporation flat nearby and says he needs a bed and furniture. John is calm and patient with him. This is George. He can't look after himself at all and his flat has to be regularly fumigated. Willie drops in to say hullo. Aged ninety, he lived in the Model for years and moved into his own flat about ten years ago. He keeps it like a new pin; he doesn't owe anyone a penny and he is spry and content. We meet Thomas, who is mildly handicapped and who stays in the Model every year for a fortnight's holidays. A dedicated movie buff, he comes to Dublin to see the latest films.

John Hayes discusses some current problems. He says the phone facility allowing people to contact the Eastern Health Board's Homeless Unit after-hours is being abused. People are waiting until evening to look for accommodation. The unit then rings around and hostels with spare beds are under pressure to take people in, even if they are unsuitable. Some cause fights, rob, create fear and tension among the older residents. Before this service, hostels had more autonomy and could make decisions about admissions for themselves. Also, those availing of the after-hours number receive free accommodation, while others have to pay.

I leave the hostel and walk to Morning Star Avenue. *En route* we meet Jimmy and Michael. Jimmy is looking particularly battered. He had TB as a child and still has a weak chest. I ask him to call to Trust and he promises he will. Michael is in good form. In his forties, he is a very heavy drinker and a bit of a charmer. A year ago his feet were so neglected that he couldn't walk. Round the corner, Eileen is sitting in her dark blue coat, scarf and black stockings. Eileen lived in Simon in the 1970s; today she is in bad form and doesn't want to talk.

In the next few minutes I meet five homeless people, including Karen who has eight children in care. I visit the *Regina Coeli* women's hostel to enquire about Kathleen. She has been run-down lately and needs a blood test. In one of the casual dormitories, women with dead-looking eyes are sitting on beds surrounded by plastic bags. A woman lies on top of a bed snoring. In another dormitory all on her own, a woman is asleep. This is Olive, whom many people and agencies have put work into over the years but to no avail.

On the street again I walk to the emergency shelter situated in a former geriatric unit in St Brendan's Hospital. It opened in 1992 after Patrick Feery died in a derelict part of the hospital nearby. The Irish army ran the shelter for a year. Their brief was to provide emergency shelter with a clean warm bed for the night, and this was achieved. Meals were provided by Civil Defence.

Since the Salvation Army took over the running of the hostel in January 1994, the brief has been interpreted somewhat differently. There have been many improvements. Garish colours have been replaced by calmer, pastel shades. New beds have been obtained. Residents now have access to a washing-machine and drier. A clothes store is being built up. Toiletries, towels and soap are available for use. A television lounge has been opened; there are books, cards and board-games to while away the hours at night. The Salvation Army brings up hot meals each evening from their kitchens in Granby Row. There is now a charge for this accommodation.

The staff have let it be known that they are available to talk, to listen and to help people in any way they can. Some have been helped to find flats. Others have been encouraged to seek help for alcohol abuse. The change has been remarkable. There are fewer fights, more trust.

I retrace my steps and call in to see Roger Grogan, brother-in-charge of the Morning Star Hostel. We discuss Derek, who has been using inappropriate levels of the heroin substitute, methadone, and Joseph, who is wetting the bed. Bed-wetting is a common but rarely discussed problem in hostels. The staff see it as a nuisance, adding to the workload. But its causes may be a kidney ailment, incontinence from long years of alcohol-abuse or, more usually, emotional and anxiety problems. Bed-wetting can be tackled and we try to bring it out into the open.

The Star offers dormitory accommodation for sixty men, many long-stay. Each resident has a bed and locker. Under Peadar's bed, white supermarket bags are packed tightly together, bursting with documentation. Peadar writes off for brochures, picks up leaflets and literature constantly and carries two crushingly heavy bundles wherever he goes.

Like all hostels, the Star has a no-drink, no-drugs rule. Roger says that people do smuggle in drink and that staff hear the bang of the bottles against the outside wall as the empties are fired out the window. Trying to screen people for drugs is impossible and these days some younger men are on drugs or need money for drugs and can rob or frighten the older men. Roger also talked about the abuse of the after-hours phone facility available through the Homeless Unit, and the problems it can cause for hostel staff and residents.

As I walk down Morning Star Avenue again, Eileen calls me over and apologises for her earlier curtness. In her mid-eighties, she tells us she has three children and one of her grandchildren is going to university. A little later I meet a group sitting on a wall drinking cider. Among them is Eleanor, in her thirties, who is mildly mentally handicapped. She was born into a homeless environment and has been in and out of psychiatric hospitals for years. Discharged that morning and on medication, Eleanor is drinking. She is easy prey sexually, and has two children in care.

I am about to leave the group when another woman asks to speak to me. This is Michelle. She tells me she is twenty-eight, has a daughter who is being cared for by her mother and a boyfriend in prison. She says she wants to stop drinking and agrees to go for residential treatment if I can organise it. She is homeless, and I give her a note for the Homeless Unit in Charles Street. She agrees to come to Trust the following day to discuss residential treatment. (She didn't turn up that day but has since made contact.)

I walk on to the day centre for homeless men in St Brendan's. It is now early afternoon. The men have had their lunch and their medication and many are lying on the grass in a drugged doze. The sight is upsetting and undignified. Inside, the centre is a cheerless place. Men sit and stare into space or look at television. I meet Tom, who talks about the painting classes the centre organises. He is enthusiastic and his eyes take on a brightness so conspicuously lacking in the others in the room.

Things are fairly quiet at the food centre in Church Street. It's a tea-and-sandwiches, not a hot-dinner day. Some men sit on in the dining-room. Down at the end a group plays cards. Jack sits at a table by himself. Aged eighty-seven, he still looks remarkably fit after a lifetime of rough living. On payday he says he buys a brandy and a vodka and has sufficient nips to make himself nice and woozy. He served in the Second World War and was on the staff of Lord Louis Mountbatten, to whom he refers by his full title.

A few tables away a younger man with a long beard sits alone. He gives me his first name but is reluctant to speak. I tell him about Trust and invite him to call. In the kitchen, presided over with quiet efficiency by Pat McMahon, food packages lie waiting to be distributed to all callers. Set up by Brother Kevin of the Capuchin Friary, the food centre is being developed in 1995 and 1996. The main door bell rings constantly for food. Nobody is refused. While the principle is admirable it gives rise to problems.

Some people take the food and sell it. Others who could afford to buy food get it here because it's free. It shows the difficulty of setting up a service for those who need it and guarding against its abuse by those who don't.

It's two o'clock and a crowd has collected outside the Homeless Unit in Charles Street. Some want a hostel place for the night; others receive their social welfare entitlement. I keep an eye on two men. Bearded, scarred, expensively dressed, they exude confidence, threat and aggression. We often receive reports of people being robbed or bullied into passing over their allowances in Charles Street as soon as they receive them.

The doors open and the crowd surges in. I go to the office to talk to the staff. They know Michelle and promise to look out for her. On the way out I notice the bearded couple hovering close to Henry, a homeless man with a heart condition who calls regularly to Trust. I go over to him and they move away.

In Brother Sebastian's tea centre on Merchant's Quay, the atmosphere is very different. I open a door from the street and climb down some steps into a a small courtyard which is bright with pale yellow walls and softened by tubs of flowers and shrubs. A few men sit outside in the sunshine. I bump into Jim, whom I haven't seen for years. Jim is a success story in that he moved, with support, from homelessness to coping in a flat on his own. He returns to the tea-centre to see old friends.

Brother Sebastian opens each day for breakfast and afternoon meals. His is one of the few centres that allows women and men to eat and socialise together, and pets are also welcome. The dining-room is attractive with good-looking furniture. News items from papers, including death notices, are pinned to the wall, very much appreciated by his callers as a way of keeping in touch with their own home town. The atmosphere is warm and there is a sense of family. Brother Sebastian greets each person by name. He says he doesn't believe there is the political will to take the caring yet radical approach that could improve the situation of the homeless. He says part of the problem is that politicians have no contact with homeless people and so promote policies in a vacuum. He believes we will always have hurt, flawed and broken people with us as part of society, and our challenge is to support them as best we can, while accepting them for who they are.

On the way to the Simon shelter on Usher's Island I pass the Dublin Mendicity Institute, a food centre in Island Street. I knock at Simon's steel-enforced front door, am vetted through an eye-hole and admitted. The entrance hall is bright and cheerful, and double doors lead from it to a sun-filled back garden. Virginia creeper climbs up a stone wall; underneath is a lawn and flower beds. The lovely garden is the work of one of the residents.

The people sitting round present a less cheerful sight. A few are reading newspapers; some stare into space. Pat lies fast asleep across a garden bench. He has put on a dreadful amount of weight. Many people have done a lot to help him but he looks as if he still doesn't care about himself.

The Simon complex comprises a shelter, a community house and a building which accommodates two work-projects paying workers £6 a day. Its aim is to give people a purpose and the opportunity to earn money for a deposit on a flat. One of the difficulties of being homeless and unemployed is the near-impossibility of changing one's circumstances, of saving money for the necessary deposit.

In one project residents are making chessboards and chessmen for sale at craft fairs. In another people are chopping and packing wood for kindling which is bought by local shops. In a dark building a woman sees me and begins to cry. Bridget is an old friend and she says I remind her of all the people no longer around. Twenty years ago she had a room in a Georgian house in Henrietta Street, but was forced out when the landlord wanted to do up the house. I also meet Eamon, who has lived in hostels for years but is now in a flat of his own. He finds it hard to manage socially and so the opportunity to work in Simon every day is important.

In the porch of the Simon community house, Tom sits in the sunshine wearing a straw hat. Now in his sixties, he has been in Simon for years. I am introduced to two young Simon volunteers. While I can understand the dependence on volunteers undertaking a six-month work contract (it was the way I first became involved with Simon), I wonder about the very young people who seem to come and go so quickly in the lives of the older homeless women and men. For many there are few people around now who know about their lives, their Dublin, their friends, their past, and that is a loss to them.

I walk to Meath Street and visit Sr Bridget in the Little Flower Social Centre, well known in Dublin as the Penny Dinner Centre. The meals now cost a little more and its image is changing. While retaining its links with homeless and elderly people, the centre is taking on a more parish-centred focus and working increasingly with local families.

Across the road the Iveagh Market is in full swing. Built by the Earl of Iveagh a hundred years ago to offer shelter in bad weather to the street traders, the market has been operating without a break since. It offers bargains in furniture, clothes, ornaments and bric-à-brac. I talk to Kathleen, Rita and Mary who have been selling in the market for years. They buy in jumble sales and offer a valuable service to people, particularly homeless people, who may lack the confidence and the cash to go into shops and are too proud to take a hand-out. We discuss Tim McDermott, who used to sit in the market every day and is now in a geriatric hospital. I suggest taking Tim out for half a day to visit the market and they are enthusiastic about the idea.

Late in the day, Paddy Gallagher and I make our way to *Brú Chaoimhín*, Cork Street, to visit Tim. It incorporates a welfare home and a geriatric hospital for men and women. Tim is in his eighties. We found him asleep in front of the television set from which a racing comment-ary blared. Seats were set out in front of the screen in cinema format. The room was dark and bare. Tim was delighted to see us and cheered up a lot as we talked.

In another room we found Bernard among a dozen men in hats and coats sitting indoors staring in silence. The air was thick with cigarette smoke, the atmosphere eerie, like stepping back in time. Bernard is from Tipper-ary, a great follower of Gaelic games who used to go to matches all round the country. We found him quiet and depressed, and we promised to visit him soon again.

We too left in a depressed state, and later voiced our concerns unofficially about *Brú Chaoimhín*. It seems to me that such places represent the hidden face of the health cutbacks. We hear about the more obvious signs of rationalisation in closed hospitals and closed wards. But this geriatric hospital offers a more silent, less visible testimony. The patients rarely receive visitors so nobody complains. But is this all we can offer our old people in Ireland in the 1990s?

(We were heartened by our next visit to Tim. There was a budgie in a cage, flowers in some of the rooms and the atmosphere was brighter and more welcoming.)

13

A Journey in Trust (2)

People in prison often have other personal family social and economic difficulties as well as criminal behaviour. For example, someone may be sentenced for larceny, but the main personal problem could be drug addiction.

Prisons can play an important role in the process of resocialisation. But we can't do it on our own. There needs to be a coordinated approach between key sections of society. For example, local authorities must provide housing, social services and support. State agencies must provide health care and education, employers must provide work opportunities.

The long-term objective and main thrust of my approach is to eliminate the ghettos and social conditions which appear to generate and stimulate crime. Achieving this requires the redirection of resources – taking from the rich and giving to the poor.

The change in mental healthcare with emphasis on community-based healthcare has been successful in many ways. However, there are shortcomings, with many, unable to cope in the community, inevitably ending up in prison.

Over 40 per cent of prisoners in Mountjoy have had some contact with the psychiatric services and 14 per cent have been in-patients.

Ideally prison should be used only as a final resort to contain those who are a real and serious threat to society. Prisons should not be used as a dumping ground for society's social misfits. The caring agencies need to do much more for this unfortunate group of people who are neither mad nor bad – but sad.

John Lonergan, governor of Mountjoy Gaol

It is early morning in Bewley's in Westmoreland Street. People with newspapers and briefcases queue up to pay for their breakfasts. There is a fire in every room, a fragrant smell of coffee wafts around. Many homeless people are on the move too at this time but many wouldn't have the confidence to come to a place like Bewley's.

I leave and turn left towards O'Connell's Bridge. As I cross the Liffey I think of what the river and the canals mean to many homeless people. They sit by them, dream, sleep by them, drink by them; sometimes it is where they meet their ends. Over the years, quite a number have died through drowning. I think of Martin, John, Mary, Joe ... Whether their deaths were accidental or deliberate, we will never know.

In O'Connell Street I pass a restaurant that used to be a snooker parlour, and where Frank, a homeless man, was permitted to sleep under a snooker table. Near the Abbey Theatre is the headquarters of the Samaritans, with whom we can have clients in common.

In Cathedral Street I visit Centre Care, a counselling service and an emigrant advice bureau, which has a welcome for the people who live in hostels or sleep rough, offering a cup of tea, warmth, space, a listening ear if needed. Secretary Lorraine Kelly says that some problems have no solutions. You have to let some people be, she says, and take them as they are.

As I walk through the Irish Life Mall, I remember when it used to be Northumberland Square, a terrace of red-brick houses. Simon had a house there in the 1970s, where one day we sat in the sunshine listening to Dr Noel Browne. The Custom House looks pale and splendid in the sunshine. Many homeless people used to sleep in its portals before being moved on. To the right is Liberty Hall, where occasionally we make representation for people in cases of disputes, unemployment or dismissal. A timely intervention may sometimes prevent someone on the margins from slipping into homelessness.

In Busáras, people are sitting on benches, waiting to meet someone or depart themselves. Here and there you spot a lone figure sitting passively, with no real urgency or expectation. Busáras is an important place in the lives of many country people who come to Dublin. Some who have lost touch with their roots sit here to see the bus arrive from their town. They get some sense of comfort, identity and connection by seeing the name of the place they came from written up on the bus. Some years ago there were many such people sitting around the terminus. Today the numbers are fewer. We have been told that officials moved them on because they were giving the place a bad image. Having said that, the staff at the bus station are very kind: they allow their washing facilities to be used by homeless people and store their belongings in the left-luggage department for safety.

There isn't time today to visit Store Street garda station; its former superintendent Joe Dowling, now Head of Community Relations, often contacted me about someone he felt needed attention. Beside the station is the City Morgue and Coroner's Court. It has been my sad task over the years to identify people found dead in tragic or ambivalent circumstances. I would make a point of meeting the relatives when they came to the inquest and telling them about their relative. Some listen and take consolation from hearing that the deceased had people who cared. Others don't want to know and cannot cope with what I would have to say.

I remember Michael who came from the west of Ireland and was found dead in the canal. He was a quiet and withdrawn personality and when I met his sisters at the inquest, they were eager to have as much information as possible. They told me that Michael was always different, always had difficulty fitting in. When he left home and severed contact, they had always worried about the knock on the door bringing bad news.

The City Morgue is run by Dublin Corporation. Coroner's Court registrar, Derek Kirwan, talks about the anguish and loneliness suffered by people who take their own lives. Many leave notes of great clarity and concern. Until the inquest, families are left in limbo, and at the inquest they have to re-live the circumstances of the death and its aftermath. Some have lots of questions not only about the death but about the wider circumstances. In almost all cases bodies are successfully identified and the staff will go to remarkable lengths to achieve this.

Out again on the street, I turn left up Buckingham Street and pass a row of small houses. It was in here I delivered one of my first babies as a Rotunda Hospital district midwife. To the right is the old fire station, a beautiful building which was once Simon's shelter. To the left a woman sweeps the path outside her door. The street is neat and trim with a sense of family life about it.

Sean MacDermott Street, in contrast, seems stark and empty, with many old buildings boarded up or showing signs of decay. I pass the back of Gloucester Street convent, once a girl's hostel, now a home for older women, and I reflect again on how many people who began life in care end up on the streets. Across the road are two Simon sheltered houses for older residents.

In the Lourdes Day Centre beside the church, there is an atmosphere of warmth and friendliness. A row of spotless tea-towels hang drying on a clothes-horse. A group of women sit having a cup of tea before starting to cook dinner for local elderly people. These are mainly volunteers, local women coming in to help their neighbours. We talk about Mary, who has been moved to a nursing-home in Clontarf. They have missed her and I promise to get them her address and hope that they will call up to see her. Over the years we have found that when people leave the social service network and are moved on, they can be very lonely. Notifying the staffs and volunteers who had contact with such people of the new address would encourage continued contact.

My eventual destination is Mountjoy Gaol. Typical

crimes now being committed by homeless people are: being drunk and disorderly, petty theft and damage to property. There may be lawful terms of imprisonment handed down for more serious crimes, but often the act of aggression, the brick through the window may arise from frustration, be a cry for help, a plea for attention.

Homeless people have great difficulty getting bail because they can't afford to pay and their homelessness can render them ineligible. Over the years I have come to see the odds stacked against law-breakers who are poor, inarticulate and homeless. I think of Joe, who was sentenced for three months for stealing 300 postcards. The same week, a government official who had defrauded his department of thousands of pounds received a suspended sentence.

In Mountjoy I meet governor John Lonergan and we discuss some of the people I have come to see. While prison is generally regarded as society's punishment, John and I agree that many homeless people almost welcome going to gaol for a while to feel safe, to receive physical care, and, if they have been on drugs, to be detoxified and get themselves together again. John says some people commit crime deliberately to come back to Mountjoy; others who are let out on temporary release, regularly come back before the time is up and ask if they may be let in again.

He says he can count on the fingers of one hand the number of prisoners from middle-class backgrounds who end up in Mountjoy. Many poor families do care and do their best but they may be unable to counter the attractions of the street and the peer group and the aimlessness imposed by unemployment, all of which can lead to crime.

As we are talking in the governor's office, a note from a prisoner is pushed under the door. John will go and see him. He says that many prisoners were never praised in their lives, never given any structure, standards, rules or regulations. He talks about the goodness in all people and says he knows of nobody, not even the so-called hard men, who haven't got some kindness in them, who haven't got some hurt in them and who haven't feelings of love for someone.

The Salvation Army Centre in Granby Row presents a very different face from other hostels for homeless people in Ireland. Built with over three million pounds in capital funding from the Department of the Environment, it opened in 1994, and is bright, comfortable, luxurious even. But a homely touch is struck immediately when we go into the office and Boom comes forward wagging his tail. He is the family pet of the centre managers, Audrey and Tom McAuley.

The hostel has over a hundred beds and provides care and supervision for residents, particularly ex-psychiatric patients and some elderly men and women transferring from other hostels whose needs were not being fully met there. There is a key worker assigned to each resident, and a housing officer, Anne Roche, who works with Dublin Corporation in finding independent accommodation for residents who would be able to move out into community.

Granby accommodation falls into two categories. The forty-seven flats in-house consist of a bedroom and bathroom. The sixty apartments grouped around a landscaped courtyard have bed-sitting room, kitchen and bathroom.

All residents pay between £40 and £60 a week, including meals, depending on circumstances and accommodation.

Southbound again, I meet Johnnie and Charlie waiting at a bus stop. They are both very drunk. A friend was buried the day before and they are still suffering the effects of his funeral. Charlie told me recently that he had a daughter who was murdered. I had not known that he had children. He was very upset when telling me, and again I reflected that for many of these men, alcohol acts as an anaesthetic to blot out sadness and failure.

I keep an eye out for Marese but she is not in her skipper near Dáil Éireann. I drop into the Mansion House to make a phone call and have a short chat with Paddy Weir, the concierge and Clare Ennis, the Lord Mayor's secretary. Over the years I have found the Mansion House to have an open and accessible attitude to all the citizens of Dublin, including its homeless ones. It is a mild afternoon, and St Stephen's Green is full of people. The park attendants are part of Trust's network. They contact us if they come across someone sleeping rough or in need of help. I find park keeper Sean Maher at lunch. He talks about many of the lonely people he sees in the course of his work. We particularly discuss Mikey, whom we are trying to persuade to come to Trust. We are slowly winning his confidence.

Michael is selling his newspapers in Grafton Street and I stop as usual for a chat. He has had his pitch for twenty years and says in that time he has seen the face of homelessness change and increase. Nowadays he says there are many young people on the street, out of home for a variety of reasons, and at risk from many dangers and difficulties.

Lunchtime Mass is being said in Clarendon Street Church. I look at the side altar and reflect how surprised the congregation would be if they knew that Marese often stores her jug-kettle behind it. I make my way to the St Vincent de Paul Hostel in Back Lane. The original hostel has been redeveloped for permanent residents and a new wing has been built on to accommodate a casual population. Both staff and residents lived with dust and machinery for months but it has been worthwhile. The new building has attracted new young volunteers to work with the experienced personnel. A few softer touches like flowers, paintings and nice colours are beginning to appear.

14

A Spiritual Experience – Paul

I arrived back to Dublin and at first was sorry I came. My brother Daniel was back also; he had split with his wife and was living in a flat in the city centre. My aunt Joan asked me to call on him, to say I had nowhere to stay, and for her sake I promised to give it a go.

It was years since Daniel and I had met. He received me with relatively poor grace but said I could stay. When I checked his kitchen I discovered his cupboards were completely bare with not an item of food. I went out and got a couple of take-aways and a more or less uneasy period with Daniel began.

I got a job in a fast-food place. Daniel was also working; so financially we were fine. Internally I was, as usual, restless. I had heard about TM (transcendental meditation) and decided to enrol for a course. I wanted convincing that it had nothing to do with religion because at this stage I had no time for God or 'bloody religion' as I called it. I got that assurance and went to my introductory session where I was taught the basic techniques, and given my mantra, the word I would say and think to bring me to a place of stillness.

Meditation worked instantly and its effect was amazing. I felt at peace; I felt I had come home. When Daniel returned that evening I was cooking the dinner. He looked at me most suspiciously and asked, 'What the fuck is wrong with you? You look different.' The next morning he woke up to find me sitting motionless in the room with my eyes closed, meditating. He leapt out of bed and shook me. He was furious when I told him what I was doing and told me in no uncertain terms to go away and do it somewhere else.

TM was initially wonderful. I loved meditating; it gave me a great peace but it was a rather selfish peace. I felt insulated from everyone and everything. Gradually my meditation grew in length and depth. I was having deep experiences. Some of them seemed to be spiritual experiences and again I went to the TM people and sought reassurance that it had nothing to do with religion. I remember my words: 'I want nothing to do with this God business.'

One day I scalded myself at work and lost my job. I needed money to live so when a man propositioned me in a pub, I went along with it. For the next two years or so I earned my living in Dublin as a male prostitute. I moved out of Daniel's flat. He was back with his wife at this stage and they were making a new life together.

So was I, a very different and secret life. I began to have regular clients. I felt quite detached and unemotional about what I was doing and grew very cynical. The number of married men who looked for homosexual experiences appalled me. I began to think there were no normal marriages.

I looked after myself, didn't get into dangerous or threatening situations. I was off all medication and I was still practising TM. It was as if nothing could touch me any more. I was finally accepting what I thought was my sexual orientation and using it to earn a living. Occasionally I asked to be or consented to being tied up and beaten. I never liked it but it was as if I was also drawn to it.

I was moving around constantly from flat to flat and finally rented a place in the city near a church. One day I noticed a sign in the porch indicating that the order was looking for people to do voluntary work in the parish. I got in touch and began to do odd jobs for the priests: some cooking in the community house and answering the phone in the office. You could say the compartmentalisation of my life was complete. Here I was – someone who did not believe in God, who had not been to Mass for years, who meditated daily with his inner consciousness and earned his living as a male prostitute – working voluntarily for the clergy! I believed TM was holding it all together.

I became friendly with one of the priests, Father B, and came to regard him as a good friend. Occasionally I attended Mass, and though I wouldn't join in the hymns or prayers, I found when I did my TM at that time it was even more powerful. One day at a small house Mass, a priest insisted on giving me Holy Communion, even though I didn't want it. I was most upset and complained to Father B, who looked at me innocently and said, 'What does it matter to you, Paul? You don't believe anyway,' whereupon I went into floods of tears.

I had almost completely lost contact with my family.

Prostitution was proving financially rewarding. At this time, a rich client asked me to live with him for a week in a city-centre hotel in order to make his ex-boyfriend jealous. I forced myself to be demonstrative in public, putting my hand on his arm and so on. The client was thrilled and so was the ex-boyfriend, who had tired of his friend and felt glad he had found someone new! So the whole idea backfired. I found myself reluctant to take the man's money and to leave him feeling so alone, so I came back and spent time with him voluntarily. It was is as if I was giving freely for a change and during a time of great cynicism, it was a turning point.

Another significant experience was the night a man picked me up and asked if he could come home with me. He couldn't go to his place because he lived in a community and it turned out he was a priest. He didn't want sex but talked about his guilt, his confusion, his problems. I felt as if I were the priest hearing his confession.

About this time I began having problems with TM. I felt I needed some kind of healing. I heard of a priest in Loughlinstown and fairly cynically, not really expecting anything, I went to see him. He said something that made me sit up: 'You do TM and Jesus doesn't want you to do TM.' He prayed with me for a little while and invited me back to a prayer meeting in Loughlinstown that evening.

I returned to town irritated and ruffled. That night, still grumbling, I found myself catching a bus back to Loughlinstown. I arrived late as I intended, stood at the back and observed. At the end of the meeting Father Richard introduced me to two men who prayed with me. They spoke about the love of God, and I responded with heavy sarcasm. I allowed them pray with me and at their request said some words of prayer myself. I left shortly after and got on the bus, telling myself I was well out of such a madhouse. But up on the top deck, I found myself talking silently to God. By the time I got off the bus, I had no doubt that God existed and cared about me.

Something had happened. But I didn't know what to do with this new experience and so put it out of my mind. I continued my meditation but instead of its leaving me full of energy, I was becoming drained and exhausted. I knew it wasn't working and gave up TM. I became miserable, depressed, without a rudder. I was still working as a prostitute but just enough to pay my rent.

I hadn't been in touch with the family for over a year. I rang Jimmy to hear that Joan was in hospital, suffering from cancer. I went to see her and was shocked by what I saw. I knew without a shadow of a doubt that she was going to die, probably within months. I tried to convey my fears to the other members of the family but they wouldn't hear of it and insisted that she was getting better.

I began to see Joan every day. She changed before my eyes and only I could see it. It got too much for me. I felt I couldn't go through her death and decided to end it all for myself first. I talked a GP into giving me a month's supply of sleeping pills, went to a chemist and got the prescription filled. I thought long and hard about finding a location to kill myself where I would not be found in time. I settled on a hostel, where I reckoned they didn't give a damn about you and you would be left to die in peace. I booked myself into a hostel and went up to my cubicle with a can of Coke and my bottle of pills. Before I began I prayed, and with hindsight my words were very important. I said, 'Jesus, save me, but only if you're going to change me.' I had had enough of my life as it was.

I began taking alternate sips of coke and mouthfuls of pills. The next thing I remember was waking up in the Meath Hospital. I had been out for thirty-six hours and I was as mad as hell at being found and rescued. After a while I staggered up to the phone to see how Joan was. I learnt that she had died while I was in the coma, that the funeral had taken place and that they had been scouring the place for me.

I put down the receiver feeling sad, relieved, empty. I was glad it was all over for her. For myself, I felt numb, strange, uncaring. I drifted back to my former lifestyle, working in the parish by day and as a prostitute by night. Then a few weeks later I found myself at a small prayer-meeting. When it was over the man who had prayed for me in Loughlinstown came to speak to me. He introduced himself as Declan and asked me to phone him. I assumed he was just another married man wanting to screw around.

The next day I phoned and he invited me over right away confirming my view that this was another client leading a double life. He offered me a cup of tea, and began to talk. I interrupted him and said, 'If you want to talk now and do it later that's OK by me but it's money up front.' Declan said, 'I don't want you here for sex, I want to tell you the Lord is delighted with you and has heard your prayer.' I thought, 'Here we go, more of the same old rubbish.' Then he said, 'The Lord heard your prayer in the hostel and will answer it. He also wants you to know that Daniel is not to blame for the course your life has taken.'

I couldn't speak I was so amazed at what I was hearing. Not then nor now, nor at any time since, has there been any rational explanation of what I learnt through Declan or how he knew what he knew about me. It could only have come through divine revelation to him, and while I am very matter-of-fact about that now, as I have had so many experiences of it over the years, I couldn't believe it at the beginning and I can understand many people having difficulty believing it also. All I can do is tell how it was.

Over the next three years or so, I saw Declan about twice a week. I grew to love and admire him and he became a father figure to me. The prostitution stopped immediately. Declan led me back gradually over a whole healing of memories. He brought up incidents and experiences from my past that I had forgotten about or suppressed for years. We prayed over these and let them go. And in the letting go, I integrated them back in myself, and gradually found myself becoming more whole. I think that's the only way I can explain it.

One of the ghosts of the past I finally confronted was my mother's death. One day I felt her presence very strongly and I mourned her. I felt that she wasn't gone, that she was still supporting me.

It was an amazing time, a honeymoon experience really, when I was learning so much. I had never been so happy. There remained the issue of homosexuality to be dealt with. Declan told me that I was not truly homosexual, that I had been living a lie all these years. But he said that a gay man would be coming into my life, that I would fall truly in love, that I would be very hurt, but it would ultimately be a life-giving experience. Some time later it happened just as he had predicted. I fell totally in love with a man called Eamonn. I was besotted with him, and for the first time in a relationship, I was the one doing all the giving. I loved him, cared for him, spent money on him that I could not afford. (Without the prostitution my lifestyle had taken a severe financial nose-dive.) Anyway, money and material things mattered very little at this time.

I expressed myself with Eamonn in a way I had never been able to before. I continued to pray during the affair and felt no great contradiction in this. Inevitably Eamonn ended the affair. I was devastated. I remember I sat on the steps outside his house for two whole nights in mute appeal for him to take me back. But when I came to myself I realised my homosexual feelings had changed. They were gone and they never returned in their original form.

This whole period was a time of intense learning for me. Of course, I made a lot of mistakes. I was full of missionary zeal, wanted to talk to everyone about Jesus and sometimes should have kept my mouth shut. I began to study the Bible and to get a lot out of it. I was going to prayer-meetings regularly and often prayed with people to good effect. But whatever good happened, whatever healings took place, they were not my doing, they were God's. I was just the channel and I knew it.

About this time I felt I wanted to become a priest. I

felt I was being called to the priesthood and heard words of invitation in my head very regularly. One day I was at a prayer-meeting when a participant said he felt someone at the meeting was being called to the priesthood and indicated a younger man I knew called John. I was very miffed and thought they had got it wrong. But one day I felt impelled to visit John and ask him if he was consider-ing the priesthood. He said he was and I told him I felt he did have a vocation. He was amazed, as he had felt in prayer that he would get confirmation of his vocation from me. So the words were not for me but for John. I was initially disappointed but again very struck at how our Lord uses us to build each other up. John was duly ordained and is currently working abroad.

I felt it was time to be reconciled with the present as well as the past. I got in touch with Jimmy, who told me my father had suffered a heart attack, was in hospital and had lost the power of speech. I had not seen my father for many years. I visited him in hospital. I told him I loved him and meant it. He could not speak, just lay there looking at me, though I know he heard me. I told him I felt he would get better, and he did. I went back out to the car to Jimmy, and cried and cried. I had thought for years that I hated my father, but I realised it wasn't true.

I visited Daniel and his wife and made my peace with them in so far as I could. The family's attitude to this new me was not unmitigated joy – in fact, they felt I had totally gone off my rocker. I wanted to talk to Daniel about the early abuse but was advised by Declan not to. Declan said that reconciliation happens only when both parties are ready for it and I must exercise some judgement on this and learn patience.

It was a wonderful time and I wanted to give something back. I was dying to do something good, noble, important. I asked Declan what could I do, if I couldn't be a priest. Declan said, 'God wants you to be as you are. He just wants you to be Paul.' I realised that was the toughest order of all.

Since that time things have never been quite the same. I think the main change is that I am never lonely. I decided to be open and not to hide any more. Already there had been too much hiding and lies. Over the years since, things have not been easy; I have made lots of mistakes, got myself into difficult situations. Trying to have a spiritual life doesn't stop the bad things happening. But it does mean that you don't have to carry them on your own.

15

WOMEN AND HOMELESSNESS

Because civil liberties are about affirming the dignity of people as autonomous human beings, homelessness is a major challenge. To be without a home is to be suspect. The homeless are easy targets. Their bodily integrity is constantly at risk. Their lives are an offence against the sacred canons of private property and consumerism. Their privacy is regularly intruded on as part of the price of being statistics in the poverty industry, their painful experiences are reduced to sociological research data.

The true test of a civilised community is how people at the margins are treated. Not only must individual liberties be defended, but society should be educated and sensitised towards a broader vision of life and living. In an area dominated by the culture of individual acquisition, home-lessness may have important lessons for us all.

Dan Sullivan, President of the Irish Council for Civil Liberties

Dear Alice,
I do hope that you will be able to come up and visit
me soon. I'm not feeling quite myself at the moment.
I think it's worrying about what I'm going to do
when I get out. It's not so bad sleeping out rough in
the summer. The winters are the worst.

This is one of many letters I received from Pauline Leonard, a homeless woman who was very special. I knew her for over fifteen years. She was in prison on a few occasions for being drunk and disorderly and from her cell would send me letters, pictures, poems, prayers, thoughts and good wishes.

I never got to know much about her background. She said her mother was Irish but that she was reared in care in England. Overall she was a happy person. She had a great sense of fun and sincere feelings of friendship and concern for many other people.

Pauline was attractive with thick dark hair. Sometimes when she came to us in Trust her hair would be dirty and matted; she could be scratched, bruised and cut from a row or a fight. She was often at the receiving end of violence from men. In Trust she would bathe, wash her hair, put on clean clothes, have a spray of perfume. Then you could see her looking at herself in the mirror and taking a pride in her appearance again.

Pauline's children were in care. She was a sensitive woman and part of her sadness was at her inability to look after her own children. She asked for them constantly and it was very important to her to know they were being well cared for. In December 1992 Pauline was found dead behind a hoarding in a derelict site in Blackhall Place. She had died from exposure and hypothermia and had lain for three days without being noticed.

Pauline's death and that of her companion Michael O'Meara, (whom we all knew as Danny Lyons) made national headlines. On the day of her funeral RTE asked me to talk about her on the *Pat Kenny Show* and reporter John Egan and I broadcast an interview from the spot where she died. Listening to the tape now, it is not surprising we sound so strained and subdued. The place was cold and bleak, the ground was littered with broken tiles, gravel, rubble, sticks and plastic bags, a place without comfort or softness. We looked down and saw the yellow chalk marks made by the gardai tracing the outlines where the bodies lay.

John asked me were there any lessons to be learned from the deaths. I felt there were and I still do. I think such a tragedy prompts all of us to ask ourselves: 'Do I know someone who is cut off and who may need help?'

Central to any study of facilities and services for homeless women is the question: how does a woman become – and remain – homeless? There are no stock answers and my observations are the product of building up individual relationships with women over many years.

Sometimes a woman wants to tell her story and then not refer to it again. Some volunteer little about themselves or their lives. We don't ask. In Trust we focus on the woman's current perception of her problem. By working with her and involving her in tackling it, we try to develop a relationship which can be part of the work to improve self-image, confidence and self-worth.

While there is no common history of female home-lessness, I have come to believe that many women who find themselves at rock bottom were subject to some overwhelming tragedy, and did not have the support, maturity, social skills or good fortune to overcome it. The following routes to female homelessness, therefore, are not mutually exclusive and any one woman may travel on a number of them.

First, there are women with personality difficulties which result from their having been brought up in care. They are often passive, lack social skills and can form interpersonal relationships only where there is a high dependency factor.

A common history would include being brought up in an orphanage and at age sixteen being placed in another institution on low pay, with board and lodging supplied. After many years of this a crisis occurs such as illness, the closure of the service, the death of an employer. As a result the woman may become permanently homeless.

Many women in hostels have spent years in psychiatric hospitals. They may have been discharged to live in flats which, after many years of dependence and medication, they are unable to manage. Many psychiatric illnesses imply difficulty in forming and maintaining supportive relationships. The result is repeated admissions to hospital – the revolving door trap. Between hospital admissions, the women spend their days in the hostel, a sad, deprived existence punctuated by eccentric behaviour or aggressive outbursts.

The next category includes women who become de-pendent on alcohol. They tend to be less acceptable in society than men; so if they become ill or homeless they may receive less support. Easing the guilt with alcohol is often the dynamic that keeps a homeless woman locked in a destructive path.

A characteristic member of the third group is the woman who, having lost her job through physical illness, may be unable to pay rent and may lose her home. Typically, she is without family, friends or supportive network. She may be single, separated or childless. She may end up in a hostel and lack the will, health or opportunities to get back to where she was. Hostel life further isolates her; she takes less care of herself and may experience intense loneliness.

The elderly woman most likely to end up in a hostel is also someone without a supportive network. She may be alone in the world, in some cases due to the death of a husband or close relative. She may be unable to live on her own, may no longer be able to afford rent and, with advancing years, may grow confused.

In spite of more tolerant attitudes, single mothers, our fifth category, are still rejected by some families and asked to leave home. Equally common is the pregnant daughter who departs because she wants to spare her family sorrow and disappointment. Some of these young mothers have poor education and no job. Unable to afford private rented accommodation or unacceptable to land-lords, they enter the hostel. Once there, the opportunities for developing a healthy lifestyle are few.

The homeless scene is increasingly encountering young women coming from violent or dysfunctional families who have had early brushes with the law. They find hostel life with its simple regulations preferable to home but they bring with them the anger, self-destructive behaviour and hurt that they experienced at home. They may drift into drug abuse, delinquency, prostitution and early pregnancy. Once they become mothers, they may stay in the hostel and so the cycle continues and becomes more entrenched.

The seventh category is a new one – that of homeless wife/partner (often with children) – which has appeared only in recent years. Out of home due to violence or other problems, they may be less visible than men and cope with their homelessness in a different way. They may stay with friends or relations short-term; then they approach the statutory bodies who may put them up in bed-and-breakfast accommodation. But this is wholly unsuitable and often very lonely. Also many establishments don't like families hanging around during the day and so a woman may be forced to walk the streets, perhaps laden down with buggy, baby, toddler and possessions. More significantly, the plight of such women often cannot be separated from the fate of their children. Hostel life, with its poverty, deprivation and lack of father figures is most damaging for children, who may become an at-risk group in society as they grow up.

Finally there are the wanderers. This grouping includes women who are not traditional travellers but single, elderly women of eccentric dress and behaviour who spend their days moving from hostel to hostel. Accurate histories are almost never available, though their wandering lifestyle may have had its origins in early mental illness. The constant movement becomes an established routine; it may give meaning to their lives and they often appear reasonably happy.

A great indictment of our attitude to homeless people is that there are no family units available in hostels. So the first thing that happens to a family when they become homeless is that officialdom splits them up. The man goes to a men's hostel; the woman and children are accommodated elsewhere.

This raises a wider question about the rights of homeless women and men to intimacy and privacy. A homeless couple seen together, perhaps sharing a bottle, are judged negatively and often moralistically. But a couple living behind closed doors do not receive the same assessment. It is as if once people have no home, society decides they have few other rights as well.

Only three hostels have an open-door policy towards women. The *Regina Coeli* Hostel has a small number of family units for women and children only (excluding fathers and teenage boys), and dormitory and single-room accommodation for women. Haven House nearby, run by the Eastern Health Board, opened in 1989 to replace the *Brú Chaoimhín* women's hostel in Cork Street, and caters for women and children. Women's Aid and other refuges provide shelter for women who flee the family home as a result of violence but accommodation is often full. Simon has accommodation for a number of women in its community houses in Usher's Island and Sean MacDermott Street.

The fact that homeless women are quieter, less disruptive socially, can mean that their problems are ignored. There are women's hostels catering for the top end of the market only, such as women coming to Dublin to work or study. Such hostels don't take people out of hospitals or people in need of care or the traditional more problem-ridden homeless woman. Their rates would exclude homeless people living on supplementary welfare. Generally speaking, there are fewer services for women. Almost all day centres and food centres seem to cater for men only.

When we began in Trust the women we worked with were often colourful, individual women, who didn't fit in and yet had a strength that helped them to cope. I'm thinking of people like Josie, who lived in Simon for many years. She would sit talking to herself, dressed all in black. She had her own seat by the fire. She left early in the morning and came back in the evening and where she was during the day we never knew.

Many homeless women then seemed freer spirits. They were allowed to live as they wanted to; there was not the great rush to rehabilitate them and force them to conform. Of course, some of them had terrible sadness and abuse in their lives. Some went around with male partners, for friendship or relationship or security. Some such couples comfort each other; others drag each other down.

Life on the streets is tough. Homeless women can lose their looks, their femininity. Some come to me for underwear, sanitary protection, toiletries and perfume, but there may be no motivation for them to look well, and if they begin drinking they often neglect their appearance badly. Or they may be under pressure if they do take care of themselves. I remember Philomena, whom I met one day wearing skirt and tights. But she was jeered at by the men for looking well and the next time I saw her she was back in the old tattered clothes. She wasn't given the permission to care and didn't have the courage to stand up for herself.

Many women we work with are not necessarily maternal. It is as if the harrowing circumstances which made them homeless in the first place have caused them to bury softer emotions in order to survive. It may be too much for them to look at what has happened in the past; such events may be submerged under layers of hurt. They don't cry much; homeless women tend to cry less than homeless men.

There are health issues, too, for homeless women. Many of them don't have a medical card; they tend not to go for preventive health screening such as cervical smear tests or breast examination. They may not know about pre-menstrual stress. They may know little about the value of exercise and a good diet, and are less likely to come across books or magazines which would have advice articles on these topics. Many middle-aged women would experience menopausal symptoms without knowing what they are, and, even if they did, they would have difficulty in asking questions about hormone replacement therapy or homoeopathic remedies.

Homeless women may be particularly prone to an inappropriate psychiatric diagnosis. In society generally it is still not so culturally acceptable for a woman to express anger, particularly violent anger. Homeless women can be angry, sad and frustrated, sometimes justifiably so, but if they are violent they may be committed to a psychiatric unit.

For some categories of young homeless women, appropriate intervention, such as a place to stay and someone to talk to, could prevent them from becoming long-term homeless. The more marginalised women that I work with also need a shelter. But it must be acceptable to them and run on lines which do not exclude them. Some women do not have the confidence to stay in comfortable and pleasant surroundings; indeed, they might believe they do not deserve a nice place. Some have serious personality problems and can't adapt to even the most casual institutional surroundings.

The same problem exists when considering a day-centre for homeless women, a service badly needed in Dublin. It is difficult for a woman to put in her day. There are many places where it may not be safe for her to sit. But no matter what resource you set up, many homeless women would not avail of it. Sometimes all we can do is befriend and give time so that change takes place slowly. There is a scope for more local services.

We also need services which are able to respond to crises in a meaningful way. One night in summer 1994 an allegedly pregnant fifteen-year-old girl was found sleeping rough in a derelict section of St Brendan's Hospital, Dublin. Originally from the west of Ireland, she emigrated with her family to England, where she spent some time in care. We first heard about Anna from Joe, who sleeps rough and who was worried about her. We made contact with Anna and her brother but it took us a week to link her up with the services. I finally brought a health board social worker to visit Anna in a field but

Anna had difficulty relating to someone she saw as an authority figure and did not cooperate. We continued to stay in touch with Anna who visited us in Trust on a number of occasions. We later heard through the grapevine that she had returned to her family. Her story illustrates the need for a flexible service which can respond to particularly difficult cases in a way that they find helpful.

In April 1995 a homeless woman, Eilish Larmour, was found dead having slept rough outside the same derelict building. Eilish was forty-one when she died and had a drink problem. She was always articulate and pleasant when she came to us in Trust. We never did discover too much about her. Eilish was a person who didn't want to discuss her bigger problems. The post-mortem was inconclusive. Foul play was not suspected, but whether she died from exposure or other causes is not clear.

Finally, I believe the role and gifts of women in developing services and in working with marginalised people are undervalued. Women bring a strength as well as a softness to this work and can often take a broader view than a male. If we are to bring love and care to people who are deprived and broken, then we must involve women. This may mean a re-education of people running services, of many professionals in church and state who have gone through a single-sex education, whose attitudes to women, positive or negative, are influenced by their own upbringing. Often the only women homeless people meet are nurses and members of religious orders, some of whom have become institutionalised themselves.

16

HEALTH AND HOMELESSNESS – AN OVERVIEW

Nobody challenges the logic and planning that brought community care into existence. There had to be a better alternative to the large, isolated, authority-wielding institutions, and keeping patients close to family support seemed a sensible alternative. The movement began in the 1950s, driven by economic rather than therapeutic motivation, and gradually it formulated into a policy.

Problems arise where bridging finance is in short supply. Institutions do not dismantle simultaneously as community services are put in place and the crossover period is more expensive to run than the original hospital-based service. This problem is at the core of service delivery everywhere.

I am convinced that a lot of illness formerly treated and sustained in hospital is now drifting on the streets unsupported and untreated and at serious risk. The fact that illness is arriving at prison location is a sad conclusion supported by a major study in Mountjoy Prison I completed in 1994. This uncovered high levels of major and disabling

illness, which had formerly been attached to the psy-
chiatric service.

I believe a lot of chronic illness also rests within the
homeless population who I think would benefit from user
friendly contact with the psychiatric services. In the past
the community tried to isolate psychiatric illness in large
distant institutions, today we are well capable of isolating
it in the community. The site of rejection may simply have
altered, while the main players – patients and staff –
continue to struggle with new locations and new pressures.

Dr Charles Smith, Clinical Director, Central Mental Hospital,
Dundrum, Dublin

Good health and homelessness seem to be a contradiction
in terms, and yet I believe some homeless people are
healthy and live happy, contented lives, with relatively few
problems or worries. They have opted out of the stresses
of conventional modern life. Like many unemployed
people, they have found other ways of feeling useful and
wanted. While it could be said that someone who sleeps
out in all weathers is not normal, what is normal? Many
have worked out a meaningful life for themselves according to their personal remit.

Such coping homelessness causes a dilemma for well-
intentioned people who want to do more to bring homeless people into line with society. I think we have to be
aware of the richness of human diversity and of the right
of people to choose their way of being healthy and coping
with the world.

On the other hand, the physical health problems of

homeless people are lifestyle-related and include bad chests, alcohol and/or drug dependency, dietary disorders, neglected feet, poor hygiene. Good health and self-esteem are linked. Being clean is more than having soap and water. If you don't feel well about yourself, you won't always seek to be clean; you may be too depressed to feel you want to be clean. You may not even feel you deserve to be sweet-smelling.

Some homeless people would ask what is the point in their being healthy? This can be a difficulty for Trust. We encourage people to be healthy, but for what? If you feel unloved or insecure, have no confidence in yourself or in the community's ability to care for you, feel you have no role, then there can be little point or value in keeping well.

The medical problems we meet today haven't changed in twenty years. However, society's so-called solutions have become much more complex. First of all, people assume that everyone has access to the health-care they need – that a medical card, for example, means access to treatment. This is not necessarily so. As well as the card you must have the will to use it. Homeless people don't always value a medical card; many of them don't have one, don't want one or lose the one they get. Furthermore, a mobile population will always have difficulty in obtaining a medical card.

GP AND OUTPATIENT SERVICE

Many GP and outpatient services are not geared to homeless people, some of whom can create disruption in a waiting-room, and there is often little understanding of their social needs. Long queues, appointments which involve hours of waiting, trudging from place to place for health entitlements . . . I often think you need to be very healthy to avail of our health services! We find people are given tablets but they don't know what they are for or how many they should take. It seems to be easier to give a prescription for medication than to give people time. Many homeless people are no different from the general population in that they do not know their rights, may not understand the medical terms used in their presence and may be too nervous to ask for an explanation. We have had people coming in to us with chest problems for which they have been prescribed several different inhalers, and using none of them.

PSYCHIATRIC SERVICES

With regard to mental and emotional health, firstly many homeless people may be labelled mentally ill, when a bit of love and understanding at the right time might have been all they needed. Should a problem arise, the immediate solution may be seen as psychiatric hospital, rather than access to a community-based service such as psychotherapy or appropriate counselling.

Second, a minority of homeless people who need the psychiatric services have problems with access. Part of this is the way they move from place to place and so are not seen as belonging to a particular catchment area. They may not be accepted by the psychiatric hospital in the area they've moved to, which gives rise to further problems. In planning services for homeless people, allowances must be made for their lifestyle.

Some people are seriously mentally ill, and fragile

communities are expected to care for them without sufficient dialogue, support or acknowledgment from appropriate agencies.

No Fixed Abode Unit (NFA)

During the 1970s Trust began making representations to the Eastern Health Board about the psychiatric needs of homeless people which, we felt, were not being met within the existing system. We had ongoing discussions with the Special Hospital Care Section of the Eastern Health Board. Finally in April 1979 a psychiatric programme for home-less people was set up in an old unit in St Brendan's Hospital. It came to be known as the No Fixed Abode Unit, NFA for short.

The criteria for selection were 'mentally ill patients below the age of sixty-five years who reside in hostels or lodging houses'. A consultant, four male day-staff and two male night-staff personnel were employed, but there were no female staff or female patients. It was recommended that one full-time community nurse and two domestics be appointed, as the possibility of moving into a new in-patient facility was imminent. Sample discharge letters were also drawn up for hostel staff on behalf of long-stay patients.

And so a programme was developed. On paper the approach seemed professional and efficient and there were great hopes for the unit. At the beginning it worked quite well. Some people went from hostels to the day-centre, where they received meals and medication, return-ing to their hostel at night. There was also a small in-patient unit, which filled up very quickly. A community nurse began to visit hostels where discharged NFA patients were on the books. In developing the NFA unit, credit is due to the consultant in charge, Dr Joe Fernandez, and his staff, who have done their best in difficult circumstances.

A crucial problem has been that, in the sixteen years since the unit opened, the large institutional mental hospitals have been closing and patients have been discharged into the community. During this time of transition the state expenditure on psychiatric services in the move from institutional care to community care has fallen considerably – a decrease of 11 per cent in real terms from 1984 to 1990 according to a well researched Simon report. So the unit would have been expected to deal with ever more patients who drift to the city, without receiving the necessary funding to carry out its brief. It has never moved from its prefab building in the grounds of St Brendan's. Hailed as the solution to mental illness among homeless people, over the years it has become a kind of dustbin. People discharged from other institutions ended up in the unit often because there was no other place for them to go. Today the NFA unit still does good work; it remains the only facility of its type for homeless people and a range of therapies is on offer. However, the unit has remained under-resourced. On reflection, for such a project to achieve its potential, it needs adequate staffing, proper funding and community services working in tandem and as a back-up, as well as ongoing dialogue with relevant voluntary agencies.

In May 1994 the then Minister for Health, Brendan Howlin, announced publicly that he was committed to introducing new mental health legislation to replace the Mental Treatment Act of 1945. He also mentioned a charter for the mentally ill, as well as research into the effectiveness of community-based services to meet the needs of the long-term mentally ill. In 1994 the Special Hospital Care Programme of the Eastern Health Board which runs the NFA unit in St Brendan's Hospital proposed a coordinated in-patient service for homeless families, community-based out-patient clinics at centres accessible to homeless people, separate day-care facilities and a community-based alcohol treatment programme for homeless people. These initiatives, if introduced, would greatly improve the workings of the NFA centre and give it the community arm it badly needs.

GENERAL HOSPITAL SERVICES

Homeless people experience special difficulties in the setting of general hospitals. They come from a twilight, isolated world where they are constantly on the move to being confined to bright rooms with lots of people. Sometimes, because there is no understanding or allowance made for them, they walk out. Or they may worry about missing their dole day, and so leave to get their money, which is very frustrating for hospital staff.

The more sophisticated our health services become, the less space there is for people who are different. Health care delivery is now planned and designed by administrators and civil servants, who are often far removed from the problems of the often bewildered patient. There is a need for a wider group, including nurses and social agencies, to be involved at the planning stage. In this situation, an organisation like Trust can be an important point of liaison between hospital staff and the homeless patient. We have established such links with some hospitals, and would welcome doing the same with others.

HOSPITAL DISCHARGE

There are also difficulties surrounding the discharge from hospitals of homeless people who may need more than medication and an out-patient appointment. We have come across people with large quantities of medication and no monitoring about how they should take it. Hospitals have a responsibility to ensure as far as possible that vulnerable homeless people are discharged into a caring environment.

There is the problem of premature hospital discharge, which often comes about because of the pressure on hospital beds. However, too often a hospital discharge note is seen as a solution in itself. Frequently, discussions take place only between community welfare officers (who have no medical or social work training) and hospital social workers. A properly planned discharge could mean that discussions should include outside agencies such as Trust, hostel staffs and community social workers.

We were recently involved in a case in which a homeless man who got around by wheelchair was discharged from a Dublin hospital. The community welfare officers in Charles Street Homeless Unit asked an overnight shelter to take him in for one night only. Three weeks later he was still spending nights in the shelter, spending his days in the street in a wheelchair managing as best he could. When he came to our notice, he was very ill, with pus oozing from both buttocks. We brought him back to the original hospital and insisted they admit him. Later we heard that after he had spent a spell in hospital, appropriate accommodation was found. It was pity it had to come later rather than sooner.

His case, not untypical, highlights the need for proper planning in hospital care and discharge. It is not sufficient for hospitals to discharge a patient into the community without first satisfying themselves that adequate care will be there for him. If this care is not available, the lack of it should be voiced by relevant hospital staffs.

In terms of healthcare and vulnerable people, we believe there is at present too great a gap between hospital and community. Many hospital staffs do not know enough about services on the ground. Further up the ladder, gaps in community services are not necessarily coming to the ears of the planners, or perhaps the planners don't hear. We believe some problems get stuck at middle management level both in hospitals and in health boards. Those who speak out (as we in Trust often do) may be ignored or labelled as troublemakers. I believe the relevant authorities should learn to listen to, and realise they can learn from, the views of voluntary agencies. If health boards expect voluntary agencies to share in the healthcare work, then they must involve them in the design and planning of programmes.

Ultimately, better planning regarding discharge, more dialogue and the provision of services to meet the real needs of people will save money and time both in the long and short term.

In theory, procedures are in place for smooth seamless

healthcare; in practice, not so. In March 1987 the Department of Health issued a circular to health-board and hospital staffs on the discharge from hospital and the aftercare of homeless people. The circular directed hospitals to put arrangements in place which would identify homeless people on admission, make their status known to social-work staff, complete a discharge form which indicated aftercare/referral action taken. The completed form should be sent to the appropriate Director of Community Care who should be notified by telephone if the homeless person does not have a medical card. The circular said that hostel staffs should be notified of the discharge of one of their residents from hospital.

Finally, it promised to carry out a review of the new procedures a year after inception, with a possible meeting of 'key people involved'. The aim of such a circular was good, and, if sensitively handled, it would have helped in the provision of an improved hospital and aftercare service for homeless people. The problem is that it was not generally implemented. While hostel staffs are generally notified by hospitals on the discharge of a resident, new residents may appear from hospital without staff knowing where they have come from or what their needs are. The daytime facilities provided specifically for ex-hospital patients among the homeless population are inadequate. Trust was never called to a special meeting to evaluate the workings of the circular. Hospital staffs are not always in a position to secure a medical card on behalf of homeless people, who often will not state they are homeless because of the stigma attached to it.

The circular is an example of officialdom at work. There is no enabling machinery. The issuing of circulars which lay down procedures is often seen as the answer to a problem. But there may be no follow-up action to see if: (a) the procedures were ever implemented; (b) they worked; (c) any improvements are needed and (d) if they were not implemented, why not? The issuing of such circulars allows government officials to claim that action has been taken when this is often no more than a bureaucratic exercise, with little change in real life.

There are day services, of course, and homeless people can avail of them. But in many cases, the clients don't fit in. I am thinking of Joe who needs somewhere to go during the day and has occasionally used a city day-hospital. But Joe is a loner. He does not like women; he is silent, withdrawn. He obviously poses a problem for staff. I would ask staffs to be particularly patient with the Joes of this world but if staff don't have the training or the understanding of what his life is like, this can be difficult.

CREATIVE SOLUTIONS

The case of Tom demonstrates what is possible. When we first met him, he was too withdrawn even to collect his social welfare entitlement and so was very neglected, malnourished and run-down. It took the combined forces of garda, psychiatric services, health-board programme manager and social welfare personnel, coordinated by Trust, to bring Tom's situation to a happy and viable solution. He now collects his social welfare benefit from Trust each week; it is sent down for him from the

Homeless Unit in Charles Street. Bonds of trust are slowly being established. This process took a long time and would have fallen apart if we had not kept with him. The present solution shows the scope for partnership between voluntary and statutory bodies, particularly when it is leavened by a little imagination and flexibility.

Not Ill, Just Inadequate

Then there is the question of the care needed for those who are socially inadequate. Robert could be described as a social misfit. Only in his fifties, he could no longer look after himself without some support. He had no home, couldn't manage hostel living, was too young for a geriatric home and unsuitable for a nursing-home. Against all advice Robert was discharged from hospital to a hostel. He gave up hope and died quite suddenly.

What Robert needed, and what many others still need, is to be accommodated in social housing support dwellings attached to hostels, near the people and places they know. This kind of approach has been initiated in a small way, but it is an expensive solution. We also need to have the vision and the will to give more support to hostel staff so that people like Robert can continue to live in the hostel that has been their home for many years. This support would need to come from hostel management committees who would actively seek and receive statutory funding to train hostel staff appropriately and to employ care staff.

Hostels and Healthcare

Ideally, hostels should be smaller. There should be someone to identify and diffuse potential crises. As presently run, hostels are not always the best places for ex-patients or for homeless people who are inadequate. These need help in matters of basic hygiene, budgeting and relationships, and this is beyond the scope of most hostels to deliver. Hostels don't always make contact with GPs or psychiatric services even when a resident needs such care. Often, a condition or an illness is not picked up at an early stage, something that would save time, suffering, even lives. As well as lack of awareness, there may be lack of authority: staffs may not have the authority from management to take appropriate action on behalf of residents. Many tell us that management does not listen to their problems.

Staff are expected to be custodians rather than carers. Many of them do their best without back-up from their management, whose vision of hostels may be very limited. We find many management committees today seem to be concerned with hostel occupancy, with numbers, rather than with the quality of the shelter they provide. Difficult people may be regarded as nuisances to be got rid of, rather than people who need care and attention. Some hostel systems actively discourage community and democracy. Residents are afraid to complain about poor food, for example, for fear of being put out. Real problems are suppressed, as happens in dysfunctional families. There is, I believe, much greater scope in hostels for building community, for giving the residents more of a say in how the organisation could and should be run.

17

An End to Running – Paul

As I began to get to know God, I needed to surround myself with people who were on a similar spiritual journey. I had given up smoking and drinking until my mentor Declan mocked mocked me gently and said I was trying to turn into a 'holy man'. I realised I had hoped to fool God and returned instead to a more normal life style. My homosexual feelings had not so much gone away as changed. I still met people to whom I was attracted but I had no desire to do anything about this.

I went to live in a city-centre hostel run by a Christian community. As soon as I entered the place I knew something was wrong. The director was a man with a strong, charismatic personality but he gave out vibes that made me wary. I had begun to trust my instinct and realise that I was learning good judgement where people were concerned.

The second night in the hostel I was awakened by raised voices. I came downstairs to find the hostel leaders praying at the tops of their voices, apparently to cast out devils from an unfortunate homeless individual. They invited me to join them. I talked to the man and said, 'I know you're going

170

along with this, because you're homeless and want a bed
for the night. But you don't have to demean yourself like
this. Get up off your knees.' I prayed with the man, simply
asking God to bless and help him, and suggested he go off
to bed. The others were not too pleased by this.

During the short time I spent with that community I
became appalled at how religion was used to manipulate
people who were vulnerable, lonely, in need of material
or emotional help. This community demonised everything.
They saw demons in alcohol, nicotine, sexuality. One day
after I had got my dole and had a few drinks, the warden
threw me out and told me I was keeping company with
demons. He showed the door to two kids from Northern
Ireland the same night, one of whom took epileptic fits.
They looked to me for help and I felt I couldn't leave
them.

We spent a few nights sleeping in an abandoned
building in Summerhill where we built a fire and kept as
warm as we could. I went along to a north-city presbytery
that took us in, providing sleeping-bags and supper. The
next morning the priest got us up early for bacon, eggs
and sausages and he gave us £3 each. The northerners
felt very threatened in a Catholic environment but this
Paul took the Peter's Pence and put it to good use.

We heard that Glencree Reconciliation Centre was
looking for volunteers and decided to give it a try. On
arrival there, we were offered gardening and outdoor
work. After a few days there was a vacancy in the kitchen.
I said I could manage it and was promptly landed with
providing lunch for fifty people that day. I panicked
initially but I had picked up a lot of catering skills in all

my years in hotels, bars and restaurants, and so I managed well and even enjoyed the work.

My two companions didn't last in Glencree but I stayed a year there. I worked six days a week for £8, plus my bed and board. I had problems dealing with some aspects of authority. I came to see that an organisation like Glencree can attract all kinds of people – many with their own needs and agendas. Billed as a centre for reconciliation, it had to involve itself in conflict resolution and this could lead to difficulties. One day I was asked to cook a meal for visiting dignitaries with what I felt were insufficient funds to buy food. I did the best I could. I bought, prepared, cooked and then walked over to the director and said, 'You can take the knife and apron and go and pray over that.' He needed a latter-day miracle of loaves and fishes to feed everyone. I left them to get on with it and went for a walk.

The centre suggested I do a catering course with CERT. During the course I lived in the centre's townhouse and they hired someone else to run the kitchen in my absence. When I returned there were immediate problems. My successor and myself did not get on. We each felt it was 'our' kitchen and neither would give way to the other. The decision was made to let me go but I wasn't told directly and was very hurt by the way the issue was handled. I left Glencree, not sure what to do with my life. I was on unemployment benefit, I was confused, rebellious, angry – with God, with life, with everyone. I was drinking a great deal and fighting with everyone.

One day I was sitting in a cafe in town when coincidentally my father and my sister Eileen sat down opposite me. I hadn't seen either of them for years and a strained, artificial conversation began between the three of us. When Eileen left us briefly I told my father I loved him. He replied, 'I love you too, son, and I'm sorry I couldn't show it to you.' I told him it wasn't his fault. We had just a few moments of real communication together and then we parted. I felt I would never see my father again and the meeting left me sad and empty.

For the next few months I began to pray for my family, particularly for my father. One night I had this strong desire to ring a friend, Conor, whom I had been in hospital with. But I did not do so. A few days later I got in touch with his flat and found that he had died the previous week. I was terribly upset and phoned my Uncle Jimmy, as I needed to talk to someone. His daughter, my niece, answered the phone and said, 'We've been looking all over for you. Your father died last week.' I went absolutely mad, I said to God, 'Fuck you, how could you do this to me? What do you want of me? I'm finished with you!'

I now entered a very dark period of my life. I lived in a hostel for three weeks and found it depressing and uncaring. I needed money to get a deposit on a flat and had a short unsuccessful stint at shoplifting, stealing and selling books. I was soon caught. The judge sentenced me to a week in prison and recommended I join a library (which I later did).

Gaol is not the worst place to be. It was boring and spiritless but I had a place to myself, I was taken care of and I didn't have to think. I can understand how prison could be a refuge for many people and how long spells in gaol can deprive people of initiative and self-confidence. Once released, I still needed money for a flat and this time, I took an honest path. I enrolled myself in some drug trials and earned £300; then I went flat hunting. I answered an ad for a flat, and though the place was awfully old-fashioned, I decided to take it.

But the elderly landlady, Mrs Roche, said she would have to think about it – would I come back tomorrow? This happened on three successive evenings. I was very angry with her and wanted to tell her what she could do with her flat but every other flat I went after, I missed by five minutes so I felt that maybe I was meant to have this flat.

And so it was to be. The next time I came back she said she would accept me as a tenant. I moved in, telling myself this was just a stopgap until I found somewhere better. Technically I had a bedsitter in which I could do my own cooking, and shared a bathroom and toilet. I kept myself to myself. During the first few nights as I was going upstairs, she came to the the door of her sitting-room and asked me in for a chat but I always refused.

The third night, after refusing her invitation, I felt impelled to go down the stairs and join her. She offered me a glass of whiskey and we began to talk. In a way it was a conversation that was to last almost ten years and was to give me more than I had thought possible. I grew to love Mrs Roche and she me. She became the mother I had lost and I the son she never had. Over the years our mutual roles grew and developed. After a relatively short time, I discovered she wasn't looking after herself properly and I began cooking for her as well as for myself. Soon, I was living in the whole house and we were helping each other. Mrs Roche would not call herself a spiritual woman, nor was she a particularly well-educated one, and yet she tore down walls in me in all kinds of ways. She welcomed my friends. I had gone to her full of a cold-hearted cynicism and gradually it all melted away. Over the years her business began getting too much for her and I used to help her run it. At this time I was working part-time at painting and decorating. We did the shopping together every Friday. I used to make it an outing for her, stopping for a drink on the way there and back. Many people thought we were mother and son and after correcting them a few times, I let it go. People would say, 'How's your mother?' and I would say, 'Fine.' I realised I had been given someone to care for and that it would be the making of me.

Mrs Roche had nieces and nephews with whom she had little contact. She was nervous of them and as she became frail, she begged me not to let them put her into a home. Finally she leased out the business. One day she fell down the stairs and had to go to hospital. I visited her every day and minded the house. One day the nieces and nephews descended and, ignoring my protests, went into her room, began rifling through her drawers, taking papers and burning them in the garden. They were looking for her will and when I attempted to intervene they told me in no uncertain terms to mind my own business.

I was desperately upset and when she came home after convalescence I told her as gently as possible what had happened. She began to be very frightened and within a few months got pneumonia and was taken into hospital again. I had no rights. The family moved her to a nursing-home and would not tell me where it was. I could not visit her. I was desperate, lonely. I stayed on in the house, trying to keep it for her, not knowing what would happen.

Six months later Mrs Roche died. Again the family didn't tell me and so prevented me from attending her funeral. At that stage, they were doing all they could to get me out of the property but I wouldn't budge. I felt they had treated her disgracefully so if I could make things as awkward for them as possible, it would be some kind of reparation on her behalf.

It was a terrible time. I missed her greatly and mourned her. I knew that my coming to live with her had extended her life but I couldn't get over how it had ended and how I had been kept from her. The family tried everything to get rid of me from the house. They changed the locks, cut off heat, light and electricity, removed the furniture piece by piece, They threatened me and harassed me. I was cold, comfortless, alone but I held on. Then one night two people came into the flat and beat me up. I don't know who they were or what their purpose was.

I was by now finally broken, ill, sore, defeated. The next day I left the house for good and went to Trust. I needed to find somewhere to stay and was told they could help. I had heard about Trust from a number of people, though I was nervous that they were do-gooders. If that was to be the case, I would be gone like a flash. I came in vary warily and nervously – and was offered a cup of tea. There was acceptance and welcome and I just sat. I was in bits; I didn't know what was going to happen to me or what I wanted to happen to me.

Later that day I met Alice Leahy. She listened; she was warm and not afraid of human contact. They asked me would I stay in a hostel until I got myself sorted out and I agreed. They fixed me up in a hostel and brought me there and introduced me. They were exactly what I needed, and I began to visit Trust regularly for a sense of family and belonging rather than for anything material. It would have been difficult to get through to me at this time. I was worn out, tense, on my guard against everyone and everything. My barriers were way up.

The hostel was the one in which I had attempted suicide all those years ago and it was strange returning to it. I lived there for three months. It was a refuge when I needed it and a great relief. For the first time in months I began to relax, and to sort my life out again. I began to see my Uncle Jim regularly. He is now an important part of my life.

Hostel life can be very lonely. It is full of ordinary people but some are suffering from extraordinary hurts. They're no better or worse than the rest of us: some are disturbed; others are good, deeply spiritual; some have been hardened and toughened by life; many are sad people.

After three months in the hostel, I felt I was able to look after myself again. I got a flat and began to learn again to live on my own. I'm still learning. I still make some mistakes and find independent living quite difficult. I've made contact with many old friends and family members over the last few years and feel a lot of old issues have been put into place. I spent an awful lot of my life running away. I don't do that any more. There was an extended family gathering last year when some relations were home from America. There I met my brother again after a gap of over a decade. He said to me, 'I'm sorry for the past.' I replied, 'If I could have picked anyone as a brother, I would have picked you.' And I meant it.

One day last summer I was sitting in St Stephen's Green when a beautiful-looking young man sat down beside me and attempted to pick me up. He said his parents were away, his house was empty and we could go there. My answer to him was: 'Don't do this. You don't know what you're getting into. If you feel ambivalent about your sexuality, go and talk to someone,' and I gave him the name of someone who could help him. I said, 'I was like you once; I thought I was homosexual and I spent half my life running away from myself with lots of suffering on the way. You're at the beginning of your life. Don't mess it up.'

18

THE 1990s

While the state should and must have responsibility for housing homeless people and for delivering mainstream housing, voluntary bodies can sometimes provide that service more flexibly and sensitively.

This is especially true of the homeless people Trust and Simon work with, some of whom have special needs. For them, housing, while essential, is often not enough. They may have medical, psychiatric and addiction problems. They may need human contact, relationships, emotional support, companionship, encouragement and affirmation.

In working with the homeless and marginalised, voluntary bodies should aim to empower people, to facilitate them to grow and develop and to take responsibility for their lives. The voluntary sector also has an important role to play in campaigning for change and social justice, critiquing government policy and challenging the values of the wider community.

There will be a continuing need for voluntary bodies which work for social justice and the elimination of poverty. There will be a continuing need for volunteers who bear witness to values such as community, inter-dependence, relationship, solidarity and mutual aid. I feel that volunteerism can be a radical political statement for the 1990s, particularly after a decade in which many western governments and economists have ruthlessly promoted rugged individualism at the expense of society and the common good.

Dick Shannon, National Director Simon Ireland

The Iveagh Trust celebrated its centenary in 1990 and as part of its celebrations it continued the refurbishment of the Iveagh Hostel. There have been great improvements. The hostel now offers 155 private bedrooms; it is a clean, bright home with pleasant colours carefully chosen. It is a credit to management that they kept the hostel open right through the renovations. The hostel is constantly booked up.

As the 1990s have progressed, we have begun to see the effects of the greatly reduced local authority building programme, a decline that began in the late 1970s and continued through the 1980s. This lack of accommodation has been exacerbated by increased family breakdown and unemployment, so that now a new face of homelessness is emerging. People who would never have contemplated homelessness are now finding themselves pushed to the margins. A 1995 Eastern Health Board report indicates that the cost of keeping mothers and children in bed and breakfast accommodation in Dublin rose from £273,000 in 1993 to £460,000 in 1994. Some people are now being put up in Grade B hotels. The cost is borne by the state but the long-term emotional cost to families is immeasur-able because whether facilities are good or poor, such locations are not home.

During the 1990s, housing legislation passed in the 1980s began to take effect. Down through the centuries laws were designed to punish homeless people rather than help them. In 1349 the first Vagrancy Laws were introduced during the Black Death in an attempt to control wandering beggars. Nineteenth-century Irish social history is littered with descriptions of the appalling conditions in the poor-houses. In 1824 over fifty British laws were consolidated in a Vagrancy Act, and extended to Ireland in 1871. In more modern Ireland, the Health Act of 1953 obliged health authorities to provide in county homes 'institutional assistance to those unable to provide shelter for themselves'. Another section of the act, however, strikes a grimmer note: 'any person' [n a county home] 'who becomes disorderly can be imprisoned for twenty-one days.' Gradually, health authorities began limiting their responsibility to provide accommodation for homeless people. The 1966 Housing Act gave priority to families and elderly people, and the single homeless person fell further behind in the queue. Between 1968 and the mid-1980s, 53.3 per cent county homes closed or reduced their night-lodging facilities for the passing homeless.

In 1983 Senator Brendan Ryan unsuccessfully intro-duced a Private Member's Bill which defined homelessness and sought to allot responsibility for homeless people to the local authorities. The Fine Gael/Labour Coalition government introduced a Housing Bill in 1985 but the

181

coalition fell before it could be enacted. In 1987 Senator Ryan reintroduced his bill, again unsuccessfully. Finally, a new Housing Act came into force on 1 January 1989.

Section 2 of the act defines a homeless person as someone living in a hospital, county home, night-shelter or other such institution unable to provide accommodation from own resources. The section has been criticised on the grounds that this definition is at the discretion of the local authority, and may not include those defined as homeless by voluntary organisations.

Section 5 gives a statutory framework for assisting voluntary bodies which provide accommodation for homeless people. This has since led to the expansion of the social housing sector. Section 9 requires local authorities to carry out a three-yearly assessment of people in need of housing (including homeless people), and, drawing on the results of this assessment, to make new schemes of letting priorities. This section too is having a beneficial effect in that single people are becoming eligible for local authority homes in a way that would not have happened in the past.

So the Housing Act has brought improvements. However, it has also shifted housing responsibility from the health board to local authorities, who tend to define needs solely in terms of housing, while health boards should take a wider brief. Indeed, many health boards do retain a responsibility for the shelter needs of homeless people as part of caring for the total person.

SOCIAL HOUSING

The trend in upgrading existing hostels has been complemented by the development of new types of supported
sheltered housing services for homeless and socially
vulnerable people. The new approach to hostel accommodation now taking place in the St Vincent de Paul, Back
Lane complex is an example of a social housing project.
Although it is still at an early stage, the health and social
needs of residents are being considered and there are plans
to introduce occupational therapy programmes in consultation with residents.

Social housing, if planned and staffed by trained
people of vision and maturity, is one answer to homelessness. Ideally, social housing and hostels should have
a client orientation, be efficiently run but not as a cold
business. There should be a built-in philosophy that staff
are not custodians and residents are treated with dignity
and given autonomy. A danger would be if hostels were
seen just as commercial undertakings with all the emphasis on bednights and occupancy. On a practical level,
it may be that organisations receive capital building
grants to provide social housing but have insufficient
funds for running costs and that this causes a problem.
Maintaining a quality service needs adequate resources.

The Salvation Army Hostel in Granby Row illustrates
that hostels need not be grubby, cheerless places. Focus
Housing Association is another example where imagin-
ative housing alternatives are becoming a reality. Simon
has had social housing in the real sense of the word for
a long time, beginning in Sarsfield Quay and now continued in Usher's Quay. A visit to the new Simon houses

in Sean MacDermott Street in 1995 was a joy. First impressions convey a sense of family. Eighteen residents are divided among the two houses; they are encouraged to put up their own posters and pictures and have their own rear garden. Long-time Simon workers Anne Burke and Pat Claffey act as unofficial house mother and father, complemented by a young voluntary and salaried staff. On my first visit there I was shown round by the residents and invited to stay to dinner. One of the residents wanted only baked beans and beetroot for his dinner and was given his choice.

An important aspect of this housing and care approach is the provision of stability and security in the lives of residents so as to enable them to come to grips with any personal problems while retaining ongoing support and healthcare. Often older people feel safer in a hostel than in a flat, and in a well-run hostel there will be a sense of community.

At present we are spending millions on subsidy to private landlords. In 1994 the supplementary welfare rent allowance cost the state £43.4m. This money was paid mainly to private landlords as a proportion of the rent on behalf of people on social welfare who can't afford to pay for their rent in full. Over 31,000 tenants were receiving rent supplements last year.

Rent supplements can create particular problems for homeless people as some landlords regard them as undesirable and don't want to supply a rent book, which makes it difficult for them to claim a subsidy.

I would like to see a standard basic basic social welfare payment right across the board and adequate local authority housing with differential rents. At present we have approximately 600-700 hostel beds in Dublin for both permanent and casual residents. We will always need hostels. We also need a good well-run shelter for thirty or so very difficult women and men who elect for a more mobile way of life. There will always be people who want to be outside of things

While the 1990s has seen the deepening of drug problems in Dublin and beyond, relatively few people on drugs make their way to Trust because they know they won't get drugs from us. Such people as we meet are linked with other agencies; we work with them to help them face their problem. As a society we cannot look at our drug problem in isolation from other problems such as poverty, deprivation and unemployment, and we are not going to be rid of our drug problem unless we are prepared to tackle causes as well as symptoms.

Other issues have surfaced in the 1990s. One is the ethical questions arising from information technology. There is increased use of this technology in the voluntary and statutory services, as elsewhere. This has facilitated the storage, proliferation and flow of information on homeless people, which raises ethical questions about privacy and security of sensitive data. The nature and extent of information on a homeless person – such as, for example, whether he has a psychiatric history or not – should be available only in so far as individual personnel need that information. We worry that some staffs are inappropriately privy to knowledge of personal details which the homeless person may not wish to reveal. We feel the ease of access to information today means that stringent standards of ethics should be set in place. Many homeless people are vulnerable and, therefore, potentially prey to exploitation. Their rights should be explained to them by those who have access to their files. Very often people feel they must answer all questions put to them, even though some may be over-personal or irrelevant. Other homeless people who are very aware of their rights may lose out on entitlements if they challenge an intrusive system.

The Homeless Persons Unit in Charles Street is run by the community welfare service. This unit, even its name, implies a response to all the social needs a homeless person may have, but its function is, in fact, primarily to provide financial support and accommodation in cases of emergency and necessity. The job of the community welfare officer is often hampered by the fact that choices of accommodation may be limited due to non-availability or special requirements, that many homeless people are very difficult to deal with and that a simple short-term response is unlikely to solve their problems.

Of its nature the community welfare service must be discretionary. A community welfare officer can, for instance, apply for commital of a homeless person whom he or she feels needs psychiatric care, a procedure rarely used but still available. An officer can influence the moving of a homeless persion from a hostel (which may have been his home for many years) to another in order to free up bed space. While it could be argued that nobody is forced to move, a strong suggestion from someone in a position of authority may be seen as an order by vulner-able client. On a day-to-day level, a community welfare officer can decide the amount of supplementary welfare allowance to pay out, can sanction or withhold the purchase of badly needed shoes or clothing.

Ideally the discretion should be positively directed towards the client and many staff do their best in very difficult circumstances. However, as the homeless population has grown, Charles Street has become a dumping ground for very many problems associated with homelessness, and frontline staff are often expected to work miracles with inadequate resources and back-up. The danger is that due to pressure of work the service might become reactive, rather than having time for reflection and a planned approach to people's needs. No one service can provide a solution to the problems of homelessness, and again we feel there is scope here for more consultation between the voluntary and statutory agencies. We in Trust work well with the community welfare officers in Charles Street. We would welcome opportunities for more consultation in planning services.

In 1993 a freephone after-hours telephone service was introduced and publicised. Its aim is to ensure that nobody has to sleep rough involuntarily in Dublin city. If people find themselves unexpectedly homeless, they can dial the freephone number which is managed by the community welfare service until 1 am, and they will be looked after. This facility is to be welcomed for certain categories of homeless people – mothers and children, for instance, who must leave home suddenly to escape family violence, or vulnerable young people out of home with nowhere to turn. The service is, however, open to abuse. People who work the system can wait until evening before asking the emergency facility to find them a bed. This

means that they don't have to pay for their accommodation. It also encourages people who could otherwise
make hostel provision for themselves not to do so. Finally,
the introduction of the service has meant that hostels are
deprived of some autonomy and often have to take people
who have been barred for intimidating other residents.

INVOLVEMENT AND RECOGNITION
In 1991 I was asked by the Archbishop of Dublin to join
the council of Crosscare, the diocesan body formerly
known as the Catholic Social Service Conference which
runs projects caring for all kinds of vulnerable groups. I
had to resign from Crosscare due to pressure of other
work. In 1992 I received a Caring Award from the Irish
Security Industry Association, nominated by the matron
of an Eastern Health Board hospital. It was encouraging
to receive such peer recognition.

In 1992 Pauline Leonard died, one of a number of
deaths which hit the headlines at the same time. The then
Lord Mayor of Dublin, Gay Mitchell, set up a working party
to look at the problems of homelessness. One of its
initiatives was a meeting at City Hall, chaired by the city
manager, to which representative groups working with
homeless people were invited. The meeting was very
useful. As a result, the Society of St Vincent de Paul
initiated a study into their services for homeless people
and produced a report with relevant recommendations.
One of those outcomes has been the development of the
Back Lane property. I am at present a member of the
management committee of the St Vincent de Paul hostel
in Back Lane.

In 1993 I was invited by consultant psychiatrist Dr Joe Fernandez to be part of his team to attend a conference in Brussels on social exclusion. The other delegates had also worked with homeless people and the debate concentrated on real human issues: people were not seen as numbers and statistics. I remember being deep in conversation with a Danish psychiatrist when someone asked if we knew each other. 'No,' he replied, 'but we know the same person.' His descriptions of the homeless people he met very much mirrored my own.

In 1993 I was the subject of an RTE radio programme *My Education* and in discussing my home and family influences I again reflected on how much of who we are is shaped by our early environment. In 1993 I received the Lord Mayor's Award for my work with homeless people in Dublin city, a case of the city fathers recognising the work of Trust. In 1993 also I was asked to join the Lord Mayor's Commission on Crime. Our report, which made very wide recommendations, was published in January 1995. In 1994 Trust made a submission to the Review Group on the Role of Supplementary Welfare Allowance in relation to housing and we subsequently met them to discuss our submission. The meeting was the first for a long time in which we sat round a table with staff from the Departments of Health, Environment and Social Welfare to discuss our problems. And I felt they listened. In June 1995, I was invited by the Department of Health to become a member of the working group on the care of teh disturbed mentally ill. Our terms of reference are to recommend a national policy for the care of this vulnerable group.

I welcome these invitations to become involved in a variety of planning bodies and working groups which have particular relevance to my work. I believe there is a need for consultation and partnership between the statutory services, social services with grassroots workers and the voluntary sector.

Health board responsibility for homeless people devolves from the Programme Manager to the Director of Community Care and through administrators to staff on the ground. There is not, as far as I am aware, a forum to allow a range of views be heard on the planning and development of the healthcare of homeless people. Part of the problem, perhaps, is that healthcare is officially compartmentalised into health-board programmes, hospitals programmes and the psychiatric services – and the health problems of homeless people are often confined, in official eyes, to psychiatric problems. This may be one reason why a comprehensive health forum for homeless people has not been not mooted. Dublin Corporation has a Housing Forum which was set up in 1992, with representation from voluntary organisations. This body stimulates debate and take decisions about policies relating to homeless people. However, because we are not involved directly in housing, we are precluded from the relevant discussion.

I would like such a forum established in the healthcare area, an acknowledgement that the health boards see the value of involving organisations like Trust in the planning and development services for marginalised people. Many people running the state services have a low appreciation of the needs of homeless people, which are more than just a bed for the night.

Part of the problem is that there isn't always a lot of value placed on voluntary input – and sometimes an organisation is judged by its size, by the number of its paid staff, by its media profile and the number of reports it writes, by its party political affiliation. Trust does not score well in any of these ways. However, I believe Trust has a contribution to make. We are the bridge between the planners and the client group who can't always express their needs; we have over twenty years' experience in working with homeless people and we are known and trusted by them in a unique way.

Whither Trust?

So is there a role for an organisation like Trust in the 1990s? Could what we have to offer be a model for other small-scale services. We recently evaluated our work as follows:

In Trust we:

- *Meet* people's needs and deal with people on a one-to-one basis
- *Treat* people as people not as numbers
- *Make* health/welfare services accessible to those who have difficulty coping with the structure through which these services are provided
- *Encourage* the services to meet and facilitate the needs of homeless people
- *Highlight* gaps in services provided by the public sector

- *Share* information with other agencies, voluntary and statutory
- *Work* closely with other agencies to improve the plight of homeless people
- *Use* a broad range of public media, churches and public representatives to get our message across
- *Provide* educational inputs to groups of doctors, nurses, public servants and others.

Above all Trust is a way of being. It is small-scale, local but dynamic. We are accessible. We are available throughout the hostel network each week, which means that those who wish to see us can do so regularly. We are small. Unlike some overcrowded GP practices we are able to give each individual a reasonable amount of time. Our ability to work as a team facilitates a greater understanding of each person's problems – and an approach to possible solutions and the possibility of follow through. We are self-questioning and constantly assess what we do. We can make progress only if we are prepared to listen to criticism and acknowledge our failures as well as our successes.

CONCLUSION

What should come out of this book? We would like a wider understanding of the needs, goodness, talents, problems of homeless people and difficulties in working with them. We would like to encourage other people to look for more creative solutions. We would like to challenge the decision-makers to take a wider view – and to consider that they may have something to learn from an organisation like Trust.

Perhaps in twenty years time someone somewhere will pose the same questions as we have done in this book. Or better still, the questions will no longer need to be asked, because effective caring answers will have been agreed, implemented and will continue to be assessed. This, of course, will in turn pose different questions – and that is the way it should be.